PRAISE FOR THE FOUR SIDES OF SANDBOX WISDOM: BUILDING RELATIONSHIPS IN AN AGE OF CHAOS, COMPLEXITY AND CHANGE.

"These easy to read books are an absolute must in every business in America. The child-like philosophy not only reminds us how far away from the simplicity of success we have driven ourselves, but also Tom gives us the path to release the forgotten from within ourselves which makes clear the path to wealth. Wealth that we can never lose begins with the building of relationships that have no other course but to flourish in every aspect of life and the lives of those we have contact with everyday. Excellent, Tom, thank you!"

— Mark Victor Hansen
    Co-creator, #1 New York Times best-selling series
    Chicken Soup for the Soul®

"Now that we are in the relationship-based era of collaborative business, *The Four Sides of Sandbox Wisdom* is a must read for anyone wanting to understand how to build successful collaborative relationships."

— Jeff Shuman
    Professor and Director of Entrepreneurial Studies at Bentley
    College, Author of *The Rhythm of Business* and co-author of
    Collaborative Communities

"I've worked with over 5,000 CEOs and many of their management teams for over a decade. I can say without a doubt that Tom's message is vital. It is profound yet simple, written in a delightful and entertaining style that is refreshing."

— Mohamed Fathelbab
    President of Forum Resources Network and
    Former Executive Director of Young Entrepreneurs' Organization

Praise for Sandbox Wisdom: *Revolutionize Your Brand with the Genius of Childhood*

"*Sandbox Wisdom* is a true gem. Tom does a remarkable job at making the importance of human connections being really what it's all about. Just when you think you know it all, read *Sandbox Wisdom*, and then read it again. An insightful and refreshing book sure to be a <u>top</u> seller."
> —— Donald E. Graham
> Chief Executive Officer, The Washington Post

"In *Sandbox Wisdom*, Tom Asacker puts us back in touch with our instincts on how to communicate to customers and employees, and gives us "ah ha" moments on how to brand and market."
> —— Ivan Seidenberg
> President and Co-CEO of Verizon Communications

"This is not another formulaic business book written with perfect hindsight about some increasingly irrelevant business model. The lessons here are fast, timeless and under your nose."
> —— Scott Bedbury
> CEO, BrandStream, Author of *A Brand New World*

"Tom Asacker always brings a fresh perspective to marketing and business. His *Sandbox Wisdom* offers wisdom from Dr. Seuss to Gandhi and practical advice from his many years of creating emotional connections between businesses and their customers."
> —— Joyce Wycoff
> Founder, Innovation Network, Author of *Mindmapping*

"An insightful and readable little book."
> ——Fred Smith,
> Founder and Chairman, FedEx

the four sides of
SANDBOX
WISDOM®

EASTSIDE

the four sides of
SANDBOX
WISDOM.

building relationships in an age
of chaos, complexity
and change

TOM ASACKER

with Erica Orloff

Eastside Publishing

This book is printed on acid-free paper.

Published by:

EASTSIDE
Eastside Publishing

P.O. Box 368
Manchester, New Hampshire 03105

ISBN: 0-9677528-1-7

Manufactured in the United States of America
March 2002
10 9 8 7 6 5 4 3 2 1
First Edition

This book is available at substantial discounts for bulk purchases.
***For information, mail to Eastside Publishing or visit the author's
home page at www.sandboxwisdom.com.***

To the young at heart.

ACKNOWLEDGEMENTS

Hugs and high-five's to my friends and

family for their input,

support, and encouragement.

I love you all.

INTRODUCTION

I threw my cup away when I saw a child
drinking from his hands at the trough.

- Diogenes

✳

*F*once read a story about a Chinese poet, who asked a Zen master to describe the teachings of Buddha.

The master answered, "Buddha's teaching is to do something good, not to do something bad."

The poet was not impressed and said, "That's pretty simple. Even a six-year-old knows that."

The master replied, "Even though a six-year-old knows it, a sixty-year-old doesn't do it."

In my first book, *Sandbox Wisdom: Revolutionize Your Brand with the Genius of Childhood*, I wrote: "The real teacher is life." New experiences—a.k.a. change—are what bring new insights, growth, tolerance, and wisdom. But the lessons of experience, like the lessons of Buddha, appear to be hidden. Otherwise, most sixty-year-olds would be jumping in rain puddles and experienced business leaders would be skipping down Wall Street.

My sincere hope is that you are not "unimpressed" by this engaging little story, and that it will help you rediscover the obvious—namely, that you don't need a *key* to success. Because the proverbial door is a creation of your adult mind. And once realized, you'll do as Fritz Perls advised and, "Lose your mind and come to your senses."

CHAPTER ONE

I am a part of all that I have met.

- Alfred, Lord Tennyson

✳

*B*ill West was just waking up, and he had the most peculiar sensation. His face felt cold and wet. He fought with this strange dream-state, half in slumber-land, half awake. Then he realized he wasn't dreaming. *Something* was in front of his face. He flicked his hand up, knowing there could only be one explanation for that *something*. Slowly he opened one eye, then the other. There sat his lovable mutt, Blue, with a note tied loosely around his neck. Bill read the note, a quote by Abraham Lincoln: "And in the end it's not the years in your life that count. It's the life in your years." *Ain't that the truth*, Bill thought. Just then, his wife poked her head into the room.

"Happy birthday!" She snickered. "Rise and shine, Birthday Boy!"

Bill groaned, then laughed. The two of them had rediscovered their sense of play in the last year. Bill had been mentored by "the greatest kid of them all," and since then, everything in his life had transformed, including his relationships with his family and friends. Even the way he greeted his birthday had changed. A year ago, he would have rather rolled over and forgotten the whole thing.

"Are you still taking the whole day off?" Connie asked, bending over to kiss him. Bill grabbed hold of her and wrestled her to the bed next to him. "Yup. A picnic, a day at the beach, the whole nine yards. I'm going to squish my feet in the sand.

And my cell phone stays right here on the dresser. Heck . . . I'm not even going to wear my watch."

"Can't wait. In the meantime, I'm fixing you breakfast."

"What? Are you feeling OK?" he laughed, pretending to take her temperature by putting his hand on her forehead. Connie was a notoriously bad cook who dreaded entering the kitchen.

"For you? Anything!" She squeezed his hand and laughed, and with that she jumped out of bed and disappeared downstairs.

Bill got up out of bed, and grinning to himself, stretched and opened the window shades to greet the day. Then he showered and threw on some comfortable clothes for the beach excursion ahead.

He and Connie ate a breakfast of blueberry pancakes, which were neither burned nor cold nor soggy. "Not only are you a brilliant teacher," he joked, "you can now add chef to your résumé."

Connie stuck her tongue out at him and went upstairs to change for their beach day. Just then, the doorbell rang, and Bill answered the door to see his mail carrier, Kate, standing on his front porch.

"Here's your mail, Bill. But you've got to see this," she said, pulling out a white envelope covered with stamps.

"What the heck . . .?" Bill asked, turning the envelope over and over in his hands. The envelope was the finest linen, very thick, and it was covered with dozens of very old stamps. The shapes, colors and denominations of the stamps varied, but they all conveyed a theme of childhood.

2

"You just don't see stamps like those every day. We hand-cancelled the back so we wouldn't ruin them. And if you don't want the envelope Bill, believe me, I'd be happy to take it off your hands. Look at this one," she smiled, pointing to a little girl doing a cartwheel.

"Sure, I don't collect stamps," Bill said as he gingerly opened the envelope and pulled out the card. He handed Kate the envelope. "Enjoy."

"Wow! Thanks Bill. Have a great day."

"I will. It's my birthday!"

"Happy birthday!"

"Thanks!"

Bill shut the door and read the card. Of course, from the stamps, he knew it could only be from one person. A person whose mission is to bring a smile to everyone else's day— Richard Falcon. The Falcon. His mentor and guru. The man who coined the phrase "Sandbox Wisdom." The man who helped him change his life.

The card gently poked fun at Bill getting another year older, and then there was a warm message and a request:

Bill,

You've faced the challenges of the last year with a real sense of purpose and wisdom. You took the inner journey and improved your life and the lives of those whom you've touched and who've touched you. Sir Rabindrananth Tagore, Nobel Prize-winning poet wrote, "Each child comes with the message that God is not yet discouraged with man." And some adults reveal it as well. Like you, Bill.

Happy birthday, and may you have a passionate and spirit-filled year. Can I also ask a favor? Can you meet me at "our place"? The old oak at the park? Next Saturday at 11:00 a.m.? Let me know if you can't make it. Otherwise, I'll see you then.

Your Friend Always,

Falcon

Bill smiled at the thought of seeing his friend next Saturday. They hadn't spoken in a couple of months—unusual for them, but Bill had been excited and busy with changes at his company. When Connie came downstairs he gave her a hug and shared the card, then they were off to his favorite place in the world—the ocean.

Driving into the park the following Saturday to meet Falcon, Bill smiled at the memories it evoked. A year ago, despite spending huge sums on management consultants, investing in technology, and analyzing spreadsheets until he was blue in the face, his company, of which he was CEO, was facing record losses. By accident—or happy coincidence . . . or fate—a friend had called at the precise moment Bill was feeling his lowest. Before Bill knew it, he was off to meet Falcon, a former CEO, a millionaire, who had retired to pursue his hobbies with passion. After meeting at the garage where Falcon restored old cars, Falcon brought Bill to his "teacher"—none other than Annie, his adorable seven-year-old granddaughter with the built-in wisdom of the ages and the sages. Through a day the three of them spent together—at an ice cream parlor, playing tag, playing in a sandbox, looking at clouds and birds and ducks . . . things most would scoff at as a waste of time—Bill had learned some of the most valuable truths he had ever known. Lately, he had begun to think he always knew them. *We were all born with them and just forgot them on the way to adulthood.*

Bill found Falcon lying under the big oak tree, gazing skyward at shapes in the clouds. Falcon heard Bill's footsteps and rose to his feet—albeit more slowly than he had a year ago. Bill still saw the twinkle in his gentle brown eyes, the sincere and compassionate smile that was his trademark, but Falcon looked . . . well, old. Older. As if he needed to be resting. The two men hugged.

"Good to see you, Bill." Falcon patted him on the back. "And I must say, a better choice of wardrobe than when we first met here."

Bill laughed, recalling his three-piece suit—and inwardly cringing at the grass stains he got all over it following a raucous game of tag. But even in that simple game of tag he had learned how business is a contact sport. He learned that leaders have to be quick on their feet and adaptive to change. To not be afraid of a few grass stains—or emotions.

"I thought I'd wear jeans and a T-shirt today. Never know with you. I could end up diving through a mud puddle!"

"I've taught you well!"

"You certainly have."

"Which brings me, Bill, to my reason for asking you to meet me here today. Not only has it been far too long, but I also have

5

a favor to ask of you. I have a friend . . . Gayle . . . a manager at a start-up company, a terrific woman. A go-getter. But her organization is in trouble. And, like you were when I first met you, with her organization in trouble, she herself is troubled personally. She thinks about this crisis all the time."

"I can certainly relate," Bill nodded. "Remember how I told you Connie used to call me a shadow husband? Even when I was home, I wasn't really home. You know what I mean?"

"Exactly. Now, normally, because I'm so fond of Gayle, I would jump at the opportunity to work with her . . . to help her break out of her mental prison like I did with you. But I'm afraid I just can't this time. My energy . . . well, I just can't give her the time and passion she deserves."

"That's too bad, Falcon. You're the best there is. If you can't help her . . ."

"Well, you see Bill, if I can't, I know someone who can. Someone who recently had a birthday. Someone who ruined a perfectly good suit here a year ago."

"Me? I can't do what you do!"

"Of course you can. Not only have you changed as a person, but you've also accomplished organizational change of a scale I don't think I've ever seen before. You're a true leader, Bill. And though I've mentored a lot of leaders over the years, very few have embraced the principles of Sandbox Wisdom in the way you have and seriously applied them to their lives and to the lives of others."

"I'm flattered. I really am. It's been a journey. It certainly isn't a journey I ever dreamed of taking, but now, of course, I see how very worthwhile it is. Critical, in fact. I can't thank you enough—or Annie—for the insights and difference you've made in my life."

Falcon smiled.

"How is that precocious and precious Annie, by the way?" Bill asked.

"Fantastic, as always! She won her class spelling bee last week."

"Good for her!"

Bill looked around the park where his lessons began. "Remember how we found you that hubcap you needed to restore your car?"

"Sure do. I was deeply touched, Bill. That couldn't have been easy to find."

"Yeah, but it seems like such a small gesture compared to what you've done for me and my company. I'd be happy to help your friend, Gayle. It would be a way of giving back. Of carrying on our relationship through another."

"Thank you, Bill. Relationships *are* what it's all about today. I've been reading everywhere that *information* is the foundation of our 'new economy.' But you and I know that we're really in the midst of a *relationship* revolution. Given the confusing amount of products and services *and* information, relationships matter more now than ever before."

"You're right, Falcon. Now is the time to create and nurture a network of mutually rewarding relationships."

"I'm so glad you see it that way, too, Bill."

"I sure do. But I don't know if I can do what you do. When I tried to transfer our experiential learning to my organization, I really struggled at first. Telling stories to my people about our time together simply didn't cut it. I finally had to take all of my notes, from my experience with you and Annie, and create a model for teaching it and providing guidance to others. But while I did that with my people at my company, I'm not sure I can create a day at the playground that would duplicate what we did."

"Bill, simply let your inner-child break through and teach without judgment, and with an open mind. Do *your* dance, and if it helps my friend Gayle . . . that's great. Wasn't that one of our important lessons with the story-telling we did?"

"Sure," Bill nodded.

Falcon started strolling toward the duck pond, and Bill strolled next to him. "'Playground,' Bill, is simply a metaphor for a place where you feel a sense of childlike wonder, connected to your inner-self. A vibrant place where you soar with vitality. Where you temporarily forget all that you know—those learned social conventions that hold you back and dampen your compassion and creativity. Isn't your company more of a playground for your people? Isn't it a place to experiment, to try new things, to stretch? An exciting place, where everyone feels connected and where they're emotionally and intellectually energized?

"Absolutely," Bill nodded.

"So, where is that place out here in the 'real world' for you?"

"I don't know Falcon. I guess it's the ocean. It's where I spent my birthday. I get there and feel myself becoming more . . . me . . . if that makes sense. I could do it at the beach, I suppose. But I'd need Annie's help. It's her genius translated to our situation that makes it all work."

"That's true, Bill. Children are our teachers. I anticipated your request and talked to her mother about it. Nina said Annie could spend a few Saturdays with you helping Gayle. And Bill? I'll be right at my garage if you need help. We can talk over anything at any time. I believe in you, Bill. You can do this and do it well."

The two men arranged to meet the following Saturday at the beach with Annie, her mother, and Gayle. Then they fed the ducks, shook hands and each headed home.

On the drive back to his house, Bill thought of how much change he had experienced. And he remembered something Einstein once said, "The problems we face cannot be solved at the level of thinking we were at when we created them." *So we need to create new ways of thinking that will support new ways of being. We must move beyond our old habits and behaviors.* Bill had moved beyond his old thinking and old ways of being. Or rather, he had moved back to a more innocent, accepting, creative time. In any event, he now had to figure out how to share his new *way* with a total stranger.

CHAPTER TWO

"Childlikeness" has to be restored with long years
of training in the art of self-forgetfulness.

-D. T. Suzuki

✳

*T*he Saturday they all planned to meet at the beach dawned spectacularly. The air was crisp and filled with the scent of the ocean, waves rippled across the sand, and the water was a deep blue. Annie squealed with delight as her grandfather pulled his gleaming Barracuda into a parking spot near the old-fashioned boardwalk. Annie, her mother, and Falcon climbed out of the car, and Falcon spotted his friend, Gayle, getting out of her car a few spots away.

The four of them visually searched the boardwalk for Bill, before Annie finally spotted him down by the water's edge. He was dressed in orange shorts and waved for them to come join him. *I hope I can convey what Sandbox Wisdom is all about,* Bill thought, as Annie, Falcon, Nina, and Gayle took off their shoes and made their way across the warm sand to where he stood, squishing his feet into the damp shoreline.

After a hug for Annie, a clap on the back for Falcon and warm greetings to Nina and Gayle, Bill directed them to a huge plaid blanket.

"A day at the beach is not complete without sandwiches and sodas and snacks. And let me tell you, these sandwiches are one of my trademarks. You're going to love 'em! Anyone hungry yet?" he grinned, sweeping his arm toward a huge cooler.

Nina smiled, "I love a man who thinks of everything, but I really have to get going. I wanted to say hello, but believe it or not, I'm running in a 10K fund raiser today and my running buddy is picking me up at the boardwalk."

"A 10K? That's fantastic!" said Bill.

Nina looked at Gayle, "Trust me, everything these guys are going to tell you about Sandbox Wisdom is going to become a way of life. A few years ago, I couldn't even run two blocks. I didn't take time to care for myself, and I certainly wasn't taking the time to nurture my relationships with others. Even with my father as a role model . . . well, I suppose that we all get in the sandbox in our own time. You know, 'when the student is ready the teacher will appear.' But trust me, once you've made the shift, you'll never go back."

Nina kneeled and gave Annie a hug. "Listen, Miss Annie, you tell Mr. West here to get you home by 8:00. I don't have to worry about him feeding you, because that cooler looks like it could feed your entire elementary school!"

"Okay Mom," Annie said. "Hey Mom! What gets wet as it dries?"

Nina rolled her eyes and smiled. "Here we go again. Okay Annie . . . I give up. What gets wet as it dries?"

Annie bent down, picked up her beach towel and beamed. "A towel!"

"You know something, Annie Cortez. You're crazy."

Annie threw her arms around Nina's neck. "You made me that way."

"I guess I did, Annie. So, Annie . . . how do you stop a fish from smelling?" Nina asked. "Put a clothespin on its nose!"

she blurted gleefully, while tickling Annie's belly. "Now have fun. I'll see you later. Bye, everyone. Bye, Dad," Nina said as she stood. "And Gayle, I guess I'll see you next Saturday. Bill has set this up for four consecutive Saturdays . . . Annie's going to love all the fresh air."

"Bye, Nina. It was great to meet you," Gayle smiled. "And good luck in your race today!"

"Can I go down and play in the sand now?" Annie asked her grandfather, after Nina left the group.

"Sure, honey."

"Wait, Annie," Bill said, reaching into a large canvas bag. He pulled out a pail and shovel, and a sieve made of bright, purple plastic.

"Purple! Oh thank you, Mr. West!" And with that Annie ran down to the shoreline where the water met the sand, and plopped down, long black braids trailing down her back, purple polka-dotted bathing suit and purple sunglasses making her an adorable—and color-coordinated—sight.

Gayle smiled, "She's such a treasure, Falcon."

Falcon smiled, a little wistfully, "She sure is, Gayle."

"You know, I am so grateful to you for arranging this, though I admit, I don't quite understand what Sandbox Wisdom is all about. I only know I need help."

"Gayle, Sandbox Wisdom was revealed to me when I was a CEO. I was hard-working, driven, closed-minded. I had an inflated ego, like most successful people. And I butted heads with everyone in my path, because I was so smart." He grinned self-deprecatingly. "I had no patience for all of you . . . for the rest of the world. And that included the very people who were dedicated to working with me."

"So when did you change? Because I can't even *picture* you being that way!"

"I'm not sure if it all happened at once. It was gradual, a process, learning that new ideas come from new sources. Fresh perspectives. I started thinking of my people more like a big family, or a community. I started thinking of where we worked as a microcosm of what life could be. Then I thought to myself, community is more than a place. It's also a state-of-mind. So I started working on *my* state-of-mind."

"Which is easier said than done," Gayle mused.

"Sure it is. But nothing worth achieving is without the growing pains of learning and change. But I'll tell you, Gayle, it all came together when Annie was born into my life."

"How?"

"I suddenly saw, up close, the most obvious elements that had been missing from my growing philosophy. Childhood is about innocence and freedom—freedom from fear, from comparison, from negativity. It's about being free from the voice in your head. It's about learning in a way where you may fail a thousand times, but it doesn't deter you."

"I think Falcon once used an analogy with me, Gayle," Bill chimed in. "When a child is learning how to walk, how many times does he or she fall down?"

"Can you count them?" Gayle asked. "My nephew's knees are perpetually bruised. My sister is thinking of getting him little kneepads!"

"Exactly," said Falcon, "but you wouldn't say to your sister, 'Hold on to him!' You wouldn't tell her, 'It's too risky!'"

"Of course not," Gayle smiled, brushing a stray strand of hair from her eyes.

"So you see, Gayle, I started watching how Annie learned, and how she interacted. I watched her laugh, from the time she was an infant to now, and I watched how she honestly and with no artifice interacted with people. And I saw that everything I'd been doing—spending money on technology and expensive consultants—wouldn't amount to anything if the people in my company, who were essentially following my lead, didn't learn how to recapture the essence of the sandbox."

"And then I," Bill said, "was led to Falcon in probably the same way you were. I was banging my head against the proverbial wall with my own company. What I thought I needed was a fresh approach. What it turned out I needed was a complete and radical shift in my awareness. Things have changed a lot in my company and my life since I first learned—or should I say *remembered*—some simple truths with Annie and Falcon as my guides. And I guess that all brings us to today."

"Well, I'm a manager, not a CEO. I don't have as much power and control as the two of you have. Can this still work for me? And what if I can't relearn how to be childlike? What if it's too late for me?"

"First Gayle," Falcon explained, "you must understand that control is an illusion. It's an albatross. It's driven by your ego's need to serve itself. You cling to it primarily to alleviate your fears—your fear of uncertainty, fear of failure, fear of being judged by others. I should know, because I tried to command and control the destiny of my company until I eventually burnt out my people and myself. Gayle, true leaders give up the need to control, come to terms with their own egos, and dedicate themselves to teaching and serving others. I'm sure you and Bill will discuss this at length."

"Falcon's right, Gayle. We like to believe otherwise. We like to believe that control is a good thing. An attribute of a strong individual. But nothing could be further from the truth. My wife has a saying that her teacher friends use to express the change most leaders, like us, need to make. She says we should stop being the 'sage on the stage,' and instead be the 'guide on the side.'"

Gayle nodded and smiled.

"And as far as it being too late for you . . . it's never too late," Bill said excitedly. "Look at Annie right now."

The three of them gazed at the nearby shoreline where Annie was decorating a sandcastle with seaweed and shells. Her attention was totally focused on her efforts, and she leaned back every few moments or so to marvel at her handiwork with a look of intense concentration on her face.

"Like molding with wet sand," Bill continued, "there are endless possibilities with people, including ourselves. We *can* make new, wonderful relationships out of our old ones. However, we must first free ourselves from our socially conditioned ways of thinking and behaving. We were molded into being who we are and in doing what we do—our 'common sense.' Learning means developing a *new* 'common sense.' You *are* what you think about all day long, Gayle, whether you know it or not. Change your belief systems and you will change your behavior . . . and your life."

"Yeah, but how can you teach me to know it, if I don't already know it by now?"

"Well, I can't promise you anything, Gayle. But after I spent the day with Annie and Falcon, I knew what had happened to me was life-changing. And I also knew that I had to figure out a way to take this new-found enthusiasm and awareness to my company, which so desperately needed to change the way it was doing business. So, I created a framework that I could use to teach our people. The way I explain it, there are four sides to the sandbox, and *all four* must be practiced simultaneously or the sand—the essence—will flow out."

"Okay, so it sounds like you're saying that there are four key principles."

"In a way, yes. Principles to live by, and not another short-lived *program*. The four sides—or principles—are Radical Awareness, Total Empathy, Childlike Honesty, and Enlightened Humor. As children, the doors to these concepts were wide open to us. So open, in fact, that we weren't even aware of them. But as we grew, our mind closed the doors and locked us into our collective belief system. So our first step, Gayle, is to help you *unlearn* all of your assumptions about how things are, and your values of what's right and wrong. You see, Gayle, knowledge is about learning something new. But we're after wisdom here—*Sandbox* Wisdom. And wisdom is all about letting go of something."

"I'm intrigued," Gayle smiled.

"Good. Each of these principles will be examined on a consecutive Saturday. And when we're done, I guarantee you that if you truly want to be, you will be transformed. Then you can take that transformation and apply it to your team at work . . . and to your life as a whole."

"Aren't you afraid that if you give away these secrets, your competitors will get a hold of them?"

"I don't worry much about my competitors anymore. Since I went through this change, I am far more concerned with my customers and employees—their desires and motivation. Besides," he shrugged, "these principles are no big secret. In fact, they're simple. It's living the principles, practicing them every day . . . that's the challenge! And even though Sandbox Wisdom is a set of principles, there is no formula. It's about personal transformation. It's about discovering *your* uniqueness. Are any two sandcastles exactly alike? Any two shells? Two starfish?"

Falcon spoke up and pointed their attention to the shoreline again, "Look at the incoming tide at the ocean's edge, Gayle. It's fluid, giving, dynamic. Like a plant or a baby. The fluid and flexible will always overcome the hard, the rigid. Change is *essential* to this philosophy, but once you grasp the principles, they become part of your unconscious. You simply embody them without thinking about them."

"Does Annie think about her creation there? Her laughter? The way she responds with affection spontaneously?" Bill asked. "Look at her. She's a master of the moment!"

"I've taught you well," Falcon responded, laughing, "Now I am more convinced than ever that you and Gayle and Annie will have a wonderful time and that you will be able to impart to Gayle the essence of our philosophy."

"Falcon, Bill, I am so grateful to you for your willingness to teach me this. I can't wait to start," Gayle smiled.

"For today, let's enjoy a picnic with Annie, and then next Saturday we'll begin." Bill stood up. "Now who's going to be the first to taste my killer ham and cheese on rye?"

Gayle and Falcon laughed as both raised their hands. Bill waved Annie back to the blanket. "Are you hungry, sweetie?"

"Starving!"

Annie sat down next to Gayle. "Look at these shells I found." The two of them bent their heads down and began poring over tiny little shells and shell fragments. Gayle oohed and ahhed over each one Annie showed her.

"Look!" Gayle exclaimed. "A piece of blue beach glass!"

Falcon looked over at Bill and smiled. "She's going to do just fine. You both are."

GAYLE'S JOURNAL

* I'm not sure I "get this" yet, but I'm willing to try.

* No two starfish are alike. So how do I discover my uniqueness?

* I already know everything I need to know, I simply have forgotten it all as I've grown into adulthood.

* Sandbox Wisdom (which I still don't totally understand) is more than a program-of-the-month. It's a state-of-mind and a way of life, and I'm going to learn the four sides: Radical Awareness, Total Empathy, Childlike Honesty, and Enlightened Humor.

* Don't be afraid of CHANGE!!

CHAPTER THREE

Let us not look back in anger or forward in fear,
but around in awareness.

- James Thurber

❋

On a windy Saturday, Gayle arrived at the beach to find Bill and Annie down by the ocean's edge. Not only was Gayle late, but she had also forgotten the plastic rake she promised Bill she would bring for Annie. She had bought the darn thing, too, but when she started running behind, she left it sitting on the desk in her front hallway. Her morning was off to a lousy start.

When she got to the beach, Annie and Bill were building small canals that ran into each other. Gayle marveled at the imagination involved. It was like a small, sandy version of Venice. Annie kept running down to the water's edge to fill her bucket with water, then she poured it into a small canal, squealing with delight as the water made its way down the waterways, joining the rest of the salty water, filling little pools and eddies.

As Gayle walked toward them, she couldn't help feeling skeptical. *Maybe it's simply the economic slowdown that's affecting my company's performance and morale.* She tried to be honest with herself. She absolutely adored Falcon. Then again, who didn't? Anyone who came in contact with him felt changed by the experience. The intensity of his attention and childlike wonder was captivating. After you left him, you wanted to be with him again. But when Falcon begged off mentoring her in favor of Bill doing it, Gayle felt disappointed.

What could she learn from Bill in these few weeks? He barely knew her or her problems. And could a CEO know what she was going through? She was on the front lines. She was dealing with morale problems in her department, in-fighting, pressures from her own boss, absenteeism, the real nitty-gritty stuff of the workplace. Gayle had her doubts that this mentoring bit was going to work at all.

"Hi Bill," Gayle mustered up a smile as she approached him. Annie was down by the shore getting yet another bucket of water.

"Hi Gayle. Are you OK . . . you're pretty late. Is everything all right?"

"Uh, huh. My mechanic promised me my car first thing this morning, but he was running behind. And then . . ."

Bill interrupted, "Gayle, I don't want to cut you off here. But, it really doesn't matter to me *why* you're late. If you say you'll be here at a certain time, you must honor that commitment. That's what creates trust. When a person says he trusts you, he's saying that he believes you to be not only sincere, but reliable as well."

Gayle felt her body stiffen. "I am reliable."

"Well, would it be better for us to change the meeting time? Make it a little later? I want us to succeed, and I'm willing to make the conditions right for you."

"No. This time is fine. It really was just a mix-up at the garage."

"Fine. I won't bring it up again, even if you continue to be late. Experience has taught me that people are not very effective as thorns. If you're motivated and you truly value our time together, you'll honor our relationship by showing up on time."

"Fair enough."

"You know Gayle, this whole thing about being late . . . about any commitment, can be just a little microcosm of the real world and our everyday dealings with everyone around us. Nothing is easier than speaking words, Gayle. And nothing is harder than living them, day in and day out."

Bill turned to watch Annie lug her bucket back to their canal system. Then she hurried down to the water again, her tiny feet leaving imprints in the sand.

"Everyone says that they value relationships—especially with their coworkers and customers. But take a look at how much time they actually spend on them. Gayle, we value what we *do* . . . period! And others value what we do as well. Say one thing and do another and we'll be like Annie's footprints there, fading into the sand. You can barely see them . . . washed away. And that's our reputation . . . washed away."

"Look, Bill . . . not to start things off on—pardon the pun—'the wrong foot,' but sometimes being late is just being late and doesn't have this bigger meaning behind it. I am really sorry we started off this way and that you've somehow gotten the wrong impression of me, but I really feel as if you're talking down to me. We're adults here, and if that's the way you want to treat me, fine . . . I can handle it. But I also have to say that I respond better to a more encouraging, supportive relationship. I'm very busy . . . I certainly didn't mean to be late."

"Believe me, I don't mean for us to start off this way either, but Gayle . . . who *isn't* busy? Your busy schedule doesn't make you any more important than anyone else. And it certainly doesn't give you an excuse for not honoring your word."

Gayle was visibly upset. "I don't get this. My mechanic made a promise to me that he couldn't keep and now this is about my *honor.* I feel like this is a classic CEO out of touch with real people and real lives, which is why I'm not sure you'll relate to my problems at work."

"Gayle, I want to relate to you. I really do. So help me understand. It sounds like you're saying that you would like me to be more accepting. Perhaps even to *motivate* you."

"Sure. Why not?"

"OK . . . let me ask you. Do you think YOU can motivate people?"

"Yes, I do." Gayle looked Bill in the eye, raising her posture a little straighter.

"Great, because I'm not so sure that I really want to come work with you next Saturday. So do me—and you—a favor . . . and MOTIVATE me!"

Gayle paused, closed her eyes briefly and took a deep breath. "I think I see where you're going with this, Bill."

"Good. Now just stay with me for a minute, okay?" Bill pointed toward the ocean. "Do you see that canal of Annie's?"

Gayle nodded.

"Go see if you can push the water out of it and back into the ocean?"

"What?"

"I know it sounds kind of dumb, but it's to make a point. Come on. Let's both try."

Gayle, with Bill at her side, got down on her knees and tried to push the water back to the sea. But other than getting sandy and wet and feeling a little stupid, she merely created a small wave, then the water returned and remained in the canal as it had started.

"And your point was?" she laughed. He was equally wet.

"My point is simply that when you try to push people from the outside—to coerce, convince, control—it may make a small or temporary change, but coerced conversion can never be trusted. It will eventually push back and return to its original position. There is no internal motivation and hence, no loyalty. True motivation is creating the right *conditions* for people to motivate—or move—themselves . . . to influence them . . . to arouse them emotionally."

"I think I understand."

"Annie," Bill beckoned to the pigtailed little girl, "You know that wooden stick we brought to carve the sand with?"

"Mmm-hmm," Annie nodded.

"Can you find it in the sand there and bring it to me?"

Annie, in a purple bathing suit with matching purple beach shoes, and purple ribbons in her hair, brought it over to Bill. He took the stick from Annie and effortlessly dragged a crevice in the wet sand directly in front of Annie's canal. The water immediately flowed into the crevice towards the ocean. Little effort. Permanent move. Whatever direction Bill moved the stick, the water followed.

He grinned at Gayle. "See. The water values movement into the crevice. It's a lot simpler than trying to *cause* it to move by pushing it, right?"

"I'd say so." Even though Gayle felt a dislike for Bill, she tried to follow his lesson.

"It's all about understanding change—especially people's resistance to change. And about the first side of our Sandbox:

Radical Awareness."

"Meaning?"

"Meaning, Gayle, that everything created in the *outside* world and with others, for instance, our relationships with friends, co-workers, family, customers, is first created in OUR *inside* world—inside of you Gayle. So the other sides of Sandbox Wisdom will not work without first understanding and practicing this principle. *Awareness* is the key ingredient."

"Awareness inside ourselves?"

"Inside ourselves *and* outside. Don't worry . . . you'll see what I mean."

"Okay. And why is it called *radical* awareness?"

"For a couple of reasons. First, it's radical, because the ability to possess childlike curiosity for the *outside* world and for the world of others, without bias or judgment, is a very rare quality in adults. Also, in order to be sensitive to what's going on around you—the *outside* world—you must be acutely aware of your *inner* world—your thoughts. Gayle, until you can appreciate how your own thoughts and, therefore, your presence alone affects the outside world and the outcomes of situations, you're doomed to unconsciously repeat dysfunctional, relationship-killing behaviors."

"Something we don't want to do, of course. Though I still don't quite follow you," Gayle said, her eyes clearly showing a little confusion.

Annie came over to them. "Did you remember my rake, Miss Gayle?"

"Sweetie, I didn't. I'm sorry. I was so upset about being late with my car at the garage that I forgot it on my desk. I'll bring it next time. I promise."

Annie looked deflated. "I understand. I'll play with my shovel." She mustered up a smile and went over to make castles.

"I feel so bad."

"You should. We have to take our promises to heart. Actually, I'm encouraged that you feel bad, Gayle. It's a sign of understanding, which is one half of the equation of the next side of our Sandbox—Total Empathy. But that's another lesson for another day. Today let's focus on understanding your inner world, especially the ego . . . what I call the *inner troll*. The ugly little creature that lives under the bridge that connects your heart and your head. To create the right conditions for others to motivate themselves, we must give up *our* ego needs, like our need to control."

"Troll, huh?"

"I heard a comedian say that once, and I really connected with it. So I decided to use the 'troll' metaphor while designing the Sandbox Wisdom model for my company with MOM."

"Mom? Your mother does this, too?"

"No," Bill chuckled. "My company has a relationship expert—a psychologist—on staff, Deanna Cunningham. We *call* her MOM. She and I talk about the troll all the time. Gayle, the other reason why we refer to it as *Radical* Awareness is because inner awareness is the only aspect of Sandbox Wisdom that small children *don't* possess. They don't have to. The troll doesn't exist for them. Society needs time to create it for them."

"We create trolls for our kids? Now, I'm really lost."

"Don't be . . . watch. Hey, Annie?" He called.

"Yes, Mr. West?"

"Tell Gayle here what happened to you the first thing this morning, when you were playing on the beach."

"Oh . . . a little boy yanked my ponytail and called me stupid. But I said that . . ." Annie flashed a broad grin and replied, in a sing-song voice, "Sticks and stones may break my bones, but words will never hurt me."

Gayle smiled, "Annie, that's very philosophical of you."

"Wait Gayle," Bill smiled. "Hear her out." Bill kneeled down to Annie's level. "And what else did you say to the little boy, Annie?"

"I told him that I felt bad for him. That he must be hurting inside."

"Thanks, Annie," Bill gave her a big hug. Then he plopped himself down in the soft sand.

"You're welcome!" Annie grinned and then turned two cartwheels as she made her way back to her canals. Gayle stood and watched her.

"Gayle," Bill looked up at Gayle with sparkling, gentle blue eyes. "'Sticks and stones' is probably the most important lesson we could ever teach our children, unfortunately, we really don't understand it ourselves. So instead, we try to perfect 'A, B, C' and '1, 2, 3'—the intellect—and 'sticks and stones'—feelings—is viewed as meaningless, childish."

"I understand it!" Gayle expressed surprise. "Words can't hurt you unless you let them."

"Gayle, with all due respect, you say you understand it, but I don't think you really do." With that, Bill instantly conjured an inquisitive look to his face and said, somewhat sarcastically, "So tell me Gayle. Why did you get so upset earlier when I said that your busy schedule doesn't give you an

EXCUSE for not honoring your word?"

For a moment, the wind seemed to still itself. And then Gayle lashed out.

"Because you questioned my integrity. That's why!"

"And HOW could you disappoint a little girl by forgetting a rake. It was one simple little thing you had to remember!"

"Look, Bill, I feel like you're bullying me!"

"There it is, Gayle! There's your inner troll. Are you aware of it now?"

"What?"

"You see, Gayle, I threatened it, and it reacted. It's a pretty simple little creature. 'Excuse' . . . 'how could you' . . . words, Gayle. Simply words. And look at your reaction. Those words hurt you."

"I guess they did."

"Sure they did. Now, let me ask you something else. What were you thinking as you drove here today? Be honest . . . were you thinking that today was going to be a waste of a morning in your very busy life?"

"Not so much that, but I was thinking that as a CEO you can't possibly get where I'm coming from, and to be honest, I still stand by that. I was also thinking that maybe it's the whisper of recession causing my problems at work and not something I can directly affect. I don't know . . . I was just doubting the effectiveness of this whole thing."

"That's your troll, Gayle. That voice in your head. Inner awareness is being conscious of that voice, AND understanding that you are *not* that voice—*not* the troll. And neither are others. This awareness allows you to observe it trying to have its way with you, and then you can ignore it when you need to. It's a mental troublemaker. Don't be a puppet to it."

"How? I mean, I hear you, I think, but how did I get this troll?"

"The troll is simply a mental image that we create as we grow up, which we believe defines who we are. It's all based on our conditioning. Take a look at Annie. She is fully in the now. Look at that sand castle of hers. She made it with love and care, like any artist or craftsperson would. She's alert and aware, but she's not 'thinking.' There is no troll telling her that she 'should do it this way,' or 'that's not good enough.' Therefore, she has no 'problems.' Problems are created in the mind. They're simply a bunch of 'what-if's and 'should of's.'"

"I think I understand," Gayle replied as she slowly lowered herself to a seated position in front of Bill.

"Gayle. Do you have any hobbies? Or, more specifically, do you have any that, when you're doing them, you feel intensely present? Free of problems?"

Gayle's face, which had registered tenseness across her brow almost since her arrival, now showed serenity. "Oil painting. Just thinking about it takes me away. Time just seems to be non-existent. I know this is going to sound really wacky or childish, but I sometimes forget to eat. I start painting on a Sunday morning and when I stop to check the time, because my stomach has growled, and it's four o'clock . . . well . . . it's like 'Where did the day go?'"

"You know why your day disappears? The troll—the voice—is shut off. It's no good at creativity. For me, I only used to get that feeling while running, but now I realize that the 'runner's high' I was seeking was inside of me all the time, not just when I was pushing into my fifth mile. All I had to do was learn how to push my troll's off-button at will—or almost at will. It takes time, however."

"I would assume so," Gayle said, "I mean, isn't that kind of what yogis do? They learn how to control the mind to a great degree?"

"Sort of. We've been conditioned over time to listen to and react to our troll. As very small children, we followed our inner signals. With no troll to mess us up, our action was spontaneous, and right! Then what happened?"

"We lost our child-like qualities?"

"Sure . . . but how? Here's how. Adults programmed us with their 'truths' of what is right, wrong, good and bad. They created our trolls for us and showed it how to judge—others and ourselves—based on these 'truths.' And so, now we have this insecure, mental troublemaker. This weak little creature that justifies its existence by worrying about the past and the future. By worrying whether or not it will be accepted. By worrying whether it will be loved. It wants to survive. It fears being rejected. It lacks the courage to be wrong, to be 'bad.' It always tries to be seen as smart, and so it defends its position. And it shuts out everything that appears to be rejection or disfavor."

"So are you blaming all of corporate America's problems, all of mine, all of everybody's problems, on bad parenting? Isn't the 'dysfunctional' label just a little overused?"

"No. This isn't about blame, Gayle. This programming wasn't done maliciously. It simply happened. We call it *living* and *learning*. With every 'don't do that' and 'don't be that way' and 'why did you do this,' the troll grew bigger and bigger. Like the little girl who was happily dancing and singing in the kitchen, while her Mom was dealing with—what she believed to be—a very stressful problem on the phone. So Mom eventually lashed out at the little girl . . . 'Be quiet! You can't sing!' And it changed the little girl forever. Her fearful troll would never let her sing again. We need to unlearn all of this rubbish."

"I hear you. My father once told me I had no grace. He said I was a klutz. Now, I won't even get on the dance floor at weddings!"

"Right! Gayle, when I was coarse with you—which was on purpose, by the way—instead of letting your troll take over—you know, 'How dare he say that to me?'—you could have chosen to see the pain and ego needs behind my words—*my* troll. My frustration. My need to be right . . . to be in control of the situation. You see, when I laid all that honor stuff on you, when I said I didn't care why you were late, it wasn't about you. It was about me. Nothing others do or say is because of you. It's because of them. Their trolls. Do you realize this? That judging and name-calling is about feeling *not* okay? It's about my troll trying to feel alive by proving that it can have an affect on you. We see people and things not as they are, but rather as *we* are."

"So *you* had the problem, not me," Gayle grinned playfully.

"Right. You need to gag the troll Gayle, and become fearless and empathetic like a small child. It's easy for them because they don't have a mind full of the past to build their identity. They have nothing to defend, because they have nothing to lose. No troll. A child is simply what she is. She doesn't wear a social mask. She's not trying to be something or impress someone. Have you ever watched a bunch of kids interact in kindergarten? There are no trolls. No one is comparing. They don't see differences. No one is one-upping, no one is trying to control. Instead, they want everyone to be happy, engaged . . . to have fun. Every child in the room is equal . . . they are true peers. Everybody is best friends."

"They hug a lot."

"Exactly, and as you learn to identify less and less with *your* troll, you'll be more at ease with people . . . with everything. You won't feel a need to judge, criticize or change people. You'll accept others. And you'll interact with them without trying to defend yourself or get for yourself, for your troll, whether your troll's need is money, status, power, whatever."

"But don't you ever have troll thoughts, Bill?"

"Absolutely. I'm not saying that you won't have them. I'm telling you to be aware—to *beware*—of them. Then they can't take you over and control you."

"So if my troll starts talking to me, should I suppress those negative thoughts?"

"No Gayle, be aware of them. Understand them. See through them. With practice, your power of inner-awareness will get deeper and deeper. You'll be like the great ocean here. Even though waves and wind and turbulence will come and go on the surface—like your negative situations and thoughts— deep down you'll remain calm and clear."

"OK. This all sounds very nice, Bill. But it's kind of touchy-feely. Can you prove any of this to me?"

"Well, you know, Falcon, without defining it, made me

aware that our economy is driven by trolls trying to find their identity and feel good through stuff and relationships. But Gayle, I have no proof. Practice it for yourself, and *you'll* be your proof."

"All right. Is that my homework assignment for the week?"

"Homework is a negative. Reminds us of something we don't usually want to do. Something we need to simply 'get done.' This is a life assignment. You'll never 'finish.' Let me tell you something else Gayle. Nothing I'm telling you is original. I'm simply imploring you to rediscover what you see and are attracted to in children."

"OK, then, how about a technique to try?"

"There is no technique. It's up to YOU to be self-aware. Socrates said that an unaware life is not worth living. And that's because you end up living a mechanical life . . . having your buttons pushed and reacting like a troll. Instead of being like our free and loving Annie."

With that, Gayle and Bill watched the little girl as she faced the sea. Her eyes were closed, her head was propped back, and her mouth was wide open. Her arms were outstretched as if she felt completely rapturous.

"Annie! What are you doing?"

"Catching the wind."

Gayle and Bill roared with laughter.

"Hey Gayle . . . feel like a bowl of hot chowder after this windy day?"

"Sure do."

"Well then, I've got a secret place where only those with a love of the salty air go. Let's head over to Hugo's Clam Shack for lunch!"

"Yahoo!" shouted Annie. She ran to Bill and he lifted her in the air in an airplane twirl. When he put her down, she said to Gayle, "Can I hold your hand?"

Despite the rough start with Bill, Gayle felt herself charmed by this enchanting little girl. "Sure, honey."

The three of them walked towards the Boardwalk, Annie in the middle holding both Gayle and Bill's hand. Every once in a while, Bill and Gayle would lift Annie into the air. Annie's smile captivated Gayle. *I sure hope I can rediscover the kid in me. I forgot how free they are,* Gayle mused. Then her stomach growled. *Chowder would be great right about now.*

GAYLE'S JOURNAL

* I'm still not sure about this whole thing.

* Radical Awareness. I need to ignore the negative voices and get back to that childlike confidence.

* I need to not be afraid to try.

* The troll. It's the voice in my head. Oh, I sure hear it a lot. My Dad was such a perfectionist, he taught it to me well.

* The economy is driven by people's trolls.

Chapter Four

Sit down before fact as a little child, be prepared to give up every preconceived notion, follow humbly wherever or whatever abysses nature leads, or you will learn nothing.

- Thomas Huxley

✳

*F*n Hugo's Clam Shack, Bill and Gayle talked. Gayle still found herself struggling with the Radical Awareness concept.

"But Bill, does giving in to the moment mean I should accept all of the negative things that happen to me?"

"Absolutely not, Gayle. You deal with them, but without being affected emotionally. You detach your 'self' from the event and deal with the situation objectively. Your situation is NOT you, Gayle. By making the situation your enemy, you simply make yourself unhappy, as well as those around you."

Just then, Bill's favorite waitress, Carol, greeted them.

"Hey there, Bill. I hope you and your two lovely friends have brought your appetites, because Hugo has cooked up the best pot of chowder today. He outdid himself!"

"Hi Carol. Can't wait to try some. Carol, this is my friend Gayle. And this . . . is Annie."

Annie grinned, minus a few front teeth.

"Wow! Did the tooth fairy visit you?

Annie nodded.

"Good for you. What a terrific smile!"

"Thank you."

"Carol? Can I ask you a question about something I saw happen here last week?"

"Sure thing, Bill."

"You were rushing over to my table, and I saw that manager over there give you a hard time. She said you weren't quick enough with an older couple a few tables away from me. But from what I saw, you were your same terrific self. Maybe a little busier than usual."

"Yeah, I remember, Bill."

"So how come after that, you weren't all flustered. Your smile was just as bright, and as I recall, you didn't let it bug you."

"Oh that. That was nothing. She's new and she sometimes yells at people when she's under pressure. But we don't let it bother us or take it personally. Anyway, if I did let her get me upset, it would only put *me* in a bad mood. We sat down and talked about it later. Things are much better now."

"Thanks, Carol. I like your way of thinking." Bill winked. "Gayle and I are engaged in some deep philosophical discussions. Anyway, Annie here will have a Shirley Temple and I'll have an iced tea, and Gayle?"

"Iced tea for me, too. Unsweetened please."

"Coming right up."

"Gayle, she may be a waitress, and some people might dismiss her way of handling customers as 'just her job,' but I respect the heck out of Carol. Do you understand how wise she is? You see, in every situation you have the choice of dealing with it, walking away from it, or of letting it go. Any other choice is insanity. During that situation, Carol decided to let it go. Your instincts will tell you what to do and when, but only if you're aware of your inner troll. Carol realizes that she's responsible for her own feelings . . . no one else is.

She didn't make any demands of her supervisor, but she did protect herself. Gayle, we spend all of our time trying to change the world—friends, associates, loved ones, bosses. But you don't have to change anything. You're in control of the world that counts the most. Your *inner* world. Your feelings. Get it?"

"I think I do."

"Don't worry, we'll spend some more time on the troll later, and on the power of feelings. For right now, let's order up a big plate of raw oysters!"

"Raw oysters? Not me!"

"Don't like the taste, huh?"

"Couldn't tell ya', Bill. I've never tried 'em. And I'm not about to start today."

Annie piped in. "Green eggs and ham, Miss Gayle."

"What? I can't say I'd like green eggs, either, Annie."

Bill winked at Annie. "Ever read Seuss's *Green Eggs and Ham,* Gayle? The good doctor is one of my favorite philosophers."

Gayle smiled. "He writes kids' stuff, right?"

"Depending on your perspective, I suppose. Annie just means, when she says 'green eggs and ham,' that you can't say you don't like something, or can't do something, until and unless you've tried."

"I vaguely remember the book. Haven't read it since grade school, though."

"Well, Sam-I-Am is a persistent fellow who eventually convinces a skeptic to try green eggs and ham. And finally, the doubter caves in, takes a bite and realizes that green eggs and ham are 'so good, so good, you see'!"

"So you think I'll like oysters, huh Sam?" Gayle asked Bill in jest.

"Maybe, but whether you do or not, this brings us to the *outside* aspect of Radical Awareness—childlike curiosity without judgment."

"Without judgment? Meaning?"

"Meaning . . . kids are naturally curious and experimental, ready to try anything. Their moment-to-moment immersion in reality is what makes them happy. It's only we ADULTS who set them up to not like things. We impose our biases. For instance, two parents have another couple over and they're trying to decide where to go to eat. In front of their child, the other couple suggests a sushi place, but the father of the child says something like 'UGH! Cold raw fish? Never!' Now the child takes her cues from Dad, and parrots that feeling. And that sort of fear can be applied to trying a new sport, meeting new people, trying anything really. We hold them back, but them? They'd try anything."

"You really think so?"

"Sure. It's the same with racism, prejudice. Do you think kids are born disliking another group of people or fearing them? One of my best friends has grown up with prejudice. Do you know what he says about racism? 'It's like family jewels that people pass along to their children.'"

"That is so profound," Gayle said, looking at Annie and thinking what a shame it would be to squash her curiosity or introduce her to prejudice. "Prejudice seems like a troll. A big troll of fear."

"You got it! Fear, Gayle. It's all about fear. Look at the oyster thing. You're afraid to try them. Yucky. And you're afraid to dance. Fear. And at work? Do you feel like you can't ever make a mistake, especially in front of the people you manage? Afraid you might look foolish?"

"Sure do. Then they won't respect me."

"Wrong. They'll respect you for trying. In the right corporate environment, mistakes are embraced because people grow from them and maybe even latch onto a vision through them. Look at kids. Children learn from mistakes and self-correct. There's no fear. There's no troll to talk them out of trying. By the way, leaders, like us, either chip away at the trolls—by encouraging, supporting, trusting, working with, and letting them practice and make mistakes—or we grow them bigger. If you trust people, you inspire a trust in themselves. They'll dare. But it's transient. It can be lost with one harsh reprimand."

Carol came over to the table. "Have you all decided?"

Gayle looked at Bill and Annie. "I think we're starting with a plate of raw oysters." She squinted her eyes and shook her head as if she couldn't believe she was hearing herself say that. "And I'll have a bowl of clam chowder for lunch."

"Me, too," Annie smiled. "With crackers."

"Make that three," Bill smiled.

"Bill, I feel like you're telling me that everything I've learned is bad. That my mind is hopelessly corrupted by my upbringing and environment, by the troll. How the heck can I unlearn an entire lifetime?"

"No. I'm really not saying that. Your mind is fluid. It's ever-changing. And you *can* change it for the good. You *can* give it new freedom, give it Radical Awareness. But you can't let the troll—all the old, learned stuff—control you. Be aware that your troll lives under your bridge, but heck, cross the bridge anyway."

Just then, a commotion came from the kitchen. Two employees crashed into each other as they both tried to enter a swinging door from opposite sides at the same time.

"Yikes! I hope no one was hurt," Gayle said.

"The kitchen, this restaurant, is old. Hugo probably needs to install a new set of doors. I saw two waiters do the same thing a few months ago."

"They need a light," Annie chimed in.

"What?" Bill and Gayle asked simultaneously.

"A light. They should set up a traffic light that goes off when people step on a mat. Yellow for slow down, green for go, red for stop."

Gayle smiled and shook her head from side to side. "That would be a great invention. That's pretty smart, Annie."

Bill nodded. "See. Creative genius. And you know, that would be easy to set up, I bet. And cheaper than remodeling the kitchen! Kids think outside the box. Even me, with all my Sandbox philosophy, think in terms of ripping apart the kitchen. Annie doesn't think that way. She thinks of something creative and yet simple. Right to the point."

Bill stared off at the kitchen. "Let me give you two a challenge. Annie Bananie with the megawatt smile vs. Gayle, the engineer. Let's see what you two can come up with. Here's the scenario: Let's say that a man wants to bring his five-foot long, one-piece fishing pole onto a bus, but the bus driver will only allow objects that are a maximum of four feet long. What can the man do?"

Annie wrinkled her brow. "Where's the man going? Is he going home? How far away does he live? Maybe he should just walk. I mean, does he have to take the bus, Mr. West?"

Bill smiled and winked at Gayle. "Kids ask a lot of questions. Like Edwin Land's daughter asking him, back in the 40's, why she couldn't see the pictures in his Brownie camera 'right away'. And what came out of that simple question? The Polaroid Land camera! Children aren't afraid of looking dumb. Adults, on the other hand, like to tell each other things. To prove our worth, our troll's worth, I guess. But it's this Radical Awareness . . . this childlike curiosity which leads to creativity. It makes us ask questions, including dumb ones. Asking questions creates dialogue, connections. And this, in turn, brings us new, valuable information. So be curious Gayle . . . ask questions . . . of everyone . . . about everything."

Annie grinned. "I got it! He could snap the pole in half and then glue it back together when he gets home. Or . . ." she wrinkled her brow in thought again, "he could bend it and carry it on. Or couldn't he hang part of it out the window?"

Bill implored Gayle, "Come on, Gayle."

"I'm thinking."

Annie chimed in again. "He can tell the bus driver that the pole is really five feet *wide*, not *long*."

Bill and Gayle both laughed uproariously. "That's a good one Annie."

But Annie's funny answer triggered an answer in Gayle's brain. "I've got it! Put the pole diagonally into a four-foot *long* by three-inch *wide* box."

"I don't understand. The pole is five feet long," Annie said, puzzled.

"Look here," Gayle smiled, excited. "I'll draw it on your placemat." With that Gayle drew a diagram in crayon on Hugo's paper placemat.

"Wow. You're really smart!" Annie grinned from ear to ear.

"Not bad, there, Gayle. But see how Annie's response, her Radical Awareness and humor, led you to be more creative. You have it in you. We all do!"

"That was fun," Gayle beamed, pleased with her answer.

"Falcon taught me that no one is as smart as everyone. Every teacher is a student and every student a teacher. At different times and under different circumstances. We need to create a flexible, creative atmosphere where ideas and questions—like Annie's—are welcomed, and people feel valued."

"Oysters!" Carol said, placing a big platter down.

"The moment of truth," Gayle smiled. She tried one, screwing up her nose in anticipation. "Hey. Not bad!"

"Thank you, thank you, Sam-I-Am," Bill laughed. The three of them ate their lunch and laughed and talked. Bill felt Gayle beginning to loosen up.

After lunch, they returned to the beach to play in the sand, and then they gathered their things. Annie skipped on the boardwalk, while Bill escorted Gayle to her car.

"Annie is amazing."

"I think so. Falcon thinks so. In fact, I can't imagine not adoring that little girl."

"She's smart as a whip, too."

"Sure is. But everyone has that childlike wisdom in them. We just get so used to our ways of thinking and doing things. We prefer sameness. That's why change is a gift, a blessing. It shakes up our current worldview. Routine deadens our senses. Newness, innocence sharpens them. You know why people hate change Gayle?"

"Because of fear?"

"In a way, yes. It's not that they fear the change. How can you fear something that you know nothing about? Rather, it's because their trolls fear losing control of the known. Or at least their illusion of control."

Gayle shook Bill's hand. "I'll see you next Saturday. On time. With the rake."

Bill smiled warmly. "I believe in you Gayle. And in this process."

After Gayle drove away, Bill settled Annie into the car, along with their cooler, blankets, and sand toys. Then he drove to Falcon's garage. He found him tinkering, as always, with one of his 'toys.'

"Grandpa!" Annie hugged him. "Is it OK if I go in the office and color?"

"Sure, Sweetpea," Falcon squeezed her hand.

When Annie was settled in the office, Falcon turned to Bill and asked, "How'd it go with Gayle today?"

"Well, I think OK. She seems to resist me. Sort of equipped with some doubt about me, the process, the truth of what I'm saying."

"Hmmm. And what did YOU think when I took you to the schoolyard to pick up Annie? Be honest with yourself. Or have you forgotten already."

Bill nodded sheepishly. "Oh yeah. I remember."

"Bill, don't try to influence Gayle, you'll just stress yourself out. Instead, simply be aware. Be present with her and her feelings. Gently dig deep. You know Bill, do you truly appreciate Gayle's worldview? As a woman, middle manager . . . under pressure to perform as well as the men, under pressure because she's a lot more expendable than you or I were or are? When you try to see where she's coming from, that will lead to mutual respect which will improve the process considerably."

"I will. But I'm still not sure she's on board."

"Remember Bill, all you can do is your 'dance.' If it helps her . . . good. If not, that's okay, too. But you must realize, as Dr. Seuss said, 'You can get help from teachers, but you are going to have to learn a lot by yourself, sitting alone in a room.'"

"As always, you're right," Bill said, patting his mentor on the shoulder. "Anyway, let me head home." He turned to walk away, and Falcon called out.

"One more thing, Bill."

"Sure."

"Take Gayle out somewhere and celebrate some small success in her development. It'll make a big difference in her morale. Everyone needs a lift!"

Bill nodded and smiled. *Falcon knows how to encourage people better than anyone. He changed my life. Now in baby steps, I can try to help someone change hers, from the inside out.*

GAYLE'S JOURNAL

* Practice Radical Awareness. Make sure the people I manage are not afraid to make suggestions. Even things that seem kind of dumb at first may inspire a truly brilliant idea in someone else.

* Don't be afraid to ask questions.

* Don't be afraid to make mistakes.

* Don't let people bug my inner troll. I can CHOOSE how to react. I really can!

* DON'T FORGET THE RAKE NEXT TIME!

CHAPTER FIVE

What do we live for, if it is not to
make life less difficult to others.

- George Eliot

✳

*G*ayle drove to the beach, the purple rake on the seat
beside her. This time, driving there, she felt more optimistic.
During the week, she had observed her troll more times than
she cared to admit. She had also seen how giving up her need
to control a bit allowed a few of her people to feel more
comfortable making suggestions. It certainly wasn't a transformation, but it was a start. Friday night, as she set TWO
alarms to make sure she didn't oversleep, she thought of Bill.
Maybe he was truly onto something. And so she took care to
make very sure that she didn't forget the rake and that she
arrived at their meeting on time.

Parking and getting out of her car, she scanned the beach
for the two of them. Spotting them near the shoreline, she
approached, trying to figure out just what the heck it was they
were doing. It was low tide, and Bill and Annie were
stomping on the hard sand near the ocean's edge.

"What ARE you two doing?" she asked, an amused smile
on her face. For a CEO, Bill certainly wasn't afraid to get wet
or . . . quite frankly . . . to look a little strange.

"We're clam hunting!" Bill said with a grin.

"Clam hunting?"

"Yup," Annie chimed in. "When we stomp hard on the sand,
sometimes a stream of water shoots up and that means that

47

there's a clam down there. Then we dig down and find it. Look in our bucket," Annie said proudly, holding out a pail full of clams.

"Impressive!" Gayle said, leaning forward to admire their finds.

"You know, even these clams can teach a lesson," Bill said.

"Why am I not surprised," Gayle joked.

"Really . . . think for a moment of the clams as your desired outcomes. Most business people are hooked on cause and effect thinking. Meaning that if they don't quickly see the effect of their efforts, there is no need to continue the process. As if there are no clams beneath the sand, because we don't see a stream of water immediately shoot up. The clams are down there. They're everywhere! But busy business people stop and try somewhere else . . . or something else. The flip side of this way of thinking is that if something *appears* to work, instead of understanding the essence of it, such as people's motivation, business people will attach themselves to the process. They'll sometimes go so far as to institutionalize it."

"Meaning?"

"They'll just keep on stomping—as if they can *cause* people or events to act in a certain way—and continue their action despite changing preferences. Many great companies, which saw their market shares erode during the 80's and 90's, fell prey to this way of thinking. Imagine if farmers acted this way. They don't immediately see the fruits of their labor, so they move on. Or, because they notice that rain appears to *cause* the plants to grow, they flood the fields with water. Relationships, like farming, are multidimensional and take time, Gayle. The marketplace, which is driven by people's feelings, is dynamic and complex. You can't let your judgments or restlessness overpower your ability to empathize with others. You have to try to understand their internal motivation . . . their preferences."

"I can't believe I'm following a clam parable, Bill, but I am." And with that, Gayle stomped hard on the sand, laughing.

Annie "high-fived" Gayle. "Isn't clam-stomping fun?"

Gayle felt a release of stress and worry, both by letting off some steam by stomping down hard on the sand, and by laughing and enjoying this precious child. "You bet it is!" she shouted, and stomped with both feet on the next spot of sand. She high-fived Annie again.

"Okay, Clam Digger, let's take our parable a bit further."

"OK. How?" Gayle asked, and stomped her feet again.

"Imagine a clam. No cheating by looking in the bucket. Just close your eyes and picture a clam in your mind. Got one?"

Gayle nodded.

"Now picture a starfish . . . now a sailboat . . . now a sunset. Pretty easy, huh? Okay, try this. Let yourself feel happy . . . now sad . . . now mad."

Gayle's brow furrowed. She opened her eyes.

"Couldn't do it, could you? That's because it's easy to grab stored images from your mind, but it takes time to process experiences and emotions. You can't rush feelings! So by all means, move quickly in business. But do so only after considering the wisdom of your childhood instincts—your heart. And the heart and motivations of others."

"I get it. Oh . . . and before I forget . . . I have a purple rake for a certain little girl. Miss Annie?"

Annie accepted the outstretched rake.

"I can use this to dig for clams!"

"Sure can. And it is purple, my Purple Princess."

Annie did a little-girl's version of a curtsy. "Yes, I AM the Purple Princess, but I am escaping from the evil witch! I'm hiding out with the Clam Digging Tribe, here with this kind gentleman, my noble Purple Knight. You mustn't tell anyone my real name."

"I promise," Gayle answered, with mock solemnity.

Annie continued stomping and digging, shouting "Eureka!" every time she found one.

"Who taught you that word, 'Eureka'?" Gayle asked.

"Mr. West. He told me the story of Archimedes who shouted out 'Eureka!' when he finally found out how to tell if a crown was pure gold by putting it in water. Isn't it the best word?"

Gayle nodded. "The enthusiasm of a child over a simple word. How unlike the troll."

"I'm glad you remembered the troll," Bill said, "because that creature is central to our philosophy. And I'm equally delighted you remembered the rake. Remember how I told you that *understanding* how Annie . . . um, the Purple Princess . . . felt when you forgot the rake was only *one* part of Total Empathy? Well, the other part is doing something about it!"

"I could never have showed up without it. I was even thinking about sleeping with it on the pillow next to me!"

Bill laughed. "Well, the next part of today's lesson will help you understand the essence of Total Empathy and how to bond with people. Like bringing the rake, returning Annie's heartfelt smile, laughing with her, making eye contact . . . you can learn how to make each connection in your life more powerful."

"Well, that's good to hear because I'm not that great at connecting with people . . . at being the life of the party."

"You've got it all wrong, Gayle. Forget about being the life of the party. People don't want to be entertained, they want to be understood!"

Gayle bent over and picked up a shell. She held it in her hand while she contemplated what Bill said.

"Does that make sense to you?"

She nodded. "I'm grateful to hear that. I was afraid that I'd have to become someone I'm not."

"Never. Sandbox Wisdom is all about revealing your authentic, childlike self, and about realizing that *everyone* possesses an inner child. But the troll silences it with fear and pain, which typically comes out as anger. If you treat these 'angry' people with kindness and a strong desire to help— Total Empathy (because you understand what the troll is all about—they'll go home and treat their children better. Now, how is *that* for making a difference? See, we often believe that only big acts can make a difference. But some of the biggest acts come from small acts of Total Empathy. Remember . . . you never know where your influence stops, Gayle."

"That's an empowering thought."

"It's a shift in consciousness! To be successful we must focus on making a difference, and not simply on making an impression or making a buck! Yes, we need 'economic wisdom,' because without access to capital and our ability to generate profits, we can't survive. But this must *not* be our purpose. We all need a purpose worth striving for. And being caring, loving, helping, expanding ourselves into the lives of others, is the one."

"Bill . . . you're sounding a little touchy-feely again," Gayle teased.

"Not really, Gayle. Think about it. Each moment is shared by every one of us, but we see it from our own, unique perspective. Total Empathy is understanding this and being able to see it from the other person's point of view—typically his or her troll view. This is the key to achieving sustainable success in business . . . in any relationship, really."

"Well, I spent a lot of time observing my troll this week. And other people's—in my department . . . at the grocery store . . . a woman at the drycleaners. I saw *it* everywhere. But trying to constantly take the troll viewpoint seems very difficult."

"It's easier than you think if you practice Total Empathy, if you shut off the 'voice' in your head. Gayle, we've become isolated in the world even though people are everywhere. Why? Because of the troll. We're egocentric. We're *living* in our heads. Instead, we need to open our ears AND our hearts. Be other-focused. Everyone, even the crankiest, crabbiest person in the world, has an innocent child in him or her that deserves respect and kindness."

"I guess I can accept that."

"Eureka!" Annie shouted. Plop went another clam into the bucket.

"Hey," said Bill, "if you're having trouble with this concept, think that every person on the planet starts out like our Annie here. Shouting for joy at discovering a daisy or a clam, or a penny on the sidewalk. Being the Purple Princess or the brave knight or the wizard. And that kid is still in there. Somewhere. If you're a puppet to your troll, you'll be taken over by troll-like emotions, suppress your inner child, and get agitated, angry, frustrated . . . the dreaded crab!"

"So now we have crabs and clams!"

He laughed. "Let me share a story with you. Something that happened today." Bill motioned for Gayle to step a little further away from Annie and he lowered his voice. "Look, I'm not saying that you will never be taken over by the troll. But when you do, realize it. Then let go of that emotion as quickly as it arose. When I picked up Annie this morning, she was upstairs getting dressed. Nina and I had a cup of coffee at the kitchen table, and we waited. Nina was worried about our day with Annie."

"Why?"

"She was worried that Annie would be crabby all day. Just before I got to Annie and Nina's, they had gotten into a bit of a fight, if you want to call it that. Annie had what Nina called a 'meltdown.' She wanted to wear her new purple sandals but couldn't find them, and she was blaming Nina. And she refused to get dressed without those gosh darn sandals. But Nina has been trying to teach Annie to put her things away neatly, to honor her responsibility in their house. So she simply informed Annie that she needed to slow down and methodically look for them, and when she found them, she had to try to remember to put them in the shoe cubbyhole Nina specifically bought for the purpose of teaching her organization skills."

"So what happened?"

"Annie started crying and having a tantrum. Her meltdown. Nina raised her voice. Annie refused to look for them . . . she was just having a 'moment,' as I like to call it. Nina yelled even louder. But moments later, when Annie came downstairs, it was if nothing had ever happened. She hugged and kissed her mom, said 'I'm sorry Mom, I love you.' and kissed her two more times. Squeezed her neck. You see, children's troll-emotions are short-lived. They express them fully, but then let them go . . . forgive. They don't hold grudges."

"Nina, in hindsight, said she hadn't been too empathetic about Annie misplacing her favorite purple sandals. And the system of organization was very new to Annie, just this week, in fact. So there were bound to be mistakes. Nina said, in reality, it was largely her fault . . . the way she reacted. Annie's reaction, her 'making up' moments with her mom, are something to emulate. Return to innocence . . . to childhood. Reclaim yourself from your troll."

"Let it go. If only it were that easy. I can try. I really can. But I saw this week how challenging it can be."

"We let silly stuff push our troll's buttons, Gayle. Your troll will create irritation automatically out of the simplest, stupidest things, which you have no control over. Think about how people whine about puddles while walking around them. Kids jump into them! Most of what we feel, we conjure up in our heads. Think about people stuck in traffic, or when we get cut off while driving. Our troll takes over. We become angry because we believe—wrongly—that someone did something *to* us. Notice the emphasis in my words there. Our troll again! Most things that happen to us have nothing to do with *us*. It has to do with *others*. We are NOT the center of everything that happens in this world. You can escape this self-centeredness by being other-focused and concerned for others. Care about their pain, their needs. It will transform your business . . . and your life."

"I can do that. I care about the people I work with already."

"I know you do. Here's another story, Gayle. Since our last meeting, I took a trip to Chicago on business. I was trying to do the trip in one day, there and back, because my wife's mother has been sick and my wife was spending a lot of time with her at the hospital. I see the stress and strain this is taking on her, and I was committed in my mind to being home each night. It was a promise I made, to myself. To our relationship. While I was in Chicago, I got a call that Dorothy, my mother-in-law, needed surgery. So I especially wanted to hurry home."

"I'm so sorry. You must have been very stressed out."

"I was. My wife, Connie, was crying on the phone. I was so frustrated because I wanted to be home at that instant. Not talking to her from a cell phone in an airport. But I had no control of the situation. Then the nightmare began. First, my return flight to my connecting airport was delayed for hours because of high winds. Then I stood in line for another hour while the airline tried to reroute me through another airline and get me home. The only way for them to get me home was to taxi me over an hour to another airport. After running to the new gate at the new airport, I found *that* flight delayed because of a mechanical problem. They eventually got me home on another flight, which put me back home at three o'clock in the morning."

"Nightmare is right."

"Exactly. But here's the interesting part of my story as it relates to Sandbox Wisdom. While I was at the final gate calmly getting my boarding pass, I noticed another passenger in line next to me whose troll had completely taken over. He was ranting and raving. He was supposed to already be home, just like me, and the flight delays were causing him to miss out on an important business meeting in the morning. But instead of the airline person empathizing—and by that I mean really listening, really making eye contact and caring—and diffusing his anger, which in his case was caused by his lack of information and control, she let *her* frustration with the situation—*her* troll—take her over. She couldn't cope with her own emotions, and thus was unable to objectively understand her customer's. She had no consideration for his well-being, his feelings. She started raising her voice and threatening to call security. Well, next thing you know . . . this guy's troll bellows, "Go ahead. Call security! None of you people know what the hell you're doing!' So her troll starts screaming for security. It threatened—I mean this—to turn into a brawl. Put the two trolls together and . . . the situation turned pretty ugly. A gentle word would have made all the difference in the world."

"What happened?"

"He ended up missing his flight—the flight I was on— because of all the shouting and nonsense. And you know what, it could have been avoided."

"How Bill? I mean, it sounds like the guy was being a real jerk."

"His *troll* was being the jerk, Gayle. That's the troll's nature. A great way to diffuse the troll's frustration—and jerk-like behavior—is to ask a caring question. The airline person could have said something like: 'Sir, I want to help you the best way that I can. Given this situation that we're in, how would you have me do that?' It would have shut down the troll temporarily while the person searched for an answer. However, it had to be heart-felt, with no hint of sarcasm."

"You're right, Bill," Gayle nodded. "I had a similar situation at work a couple of weeks ago. Not as extreme. I yelled at someone for being late with a report and then she yelled at me, and it escalated into personal criticisms. In hindsight, I could have defused it all by listening to what was going on with the report, why she was having trouble making the numbers work."

"Gayle, the most difficult thing in the world is to really listen, fully with empathy and respect. We're in such a hurry, or we're trying so hard to convince others . . . to fix things, that we don't simply listen with love in our hearts. Listening and asking questions are what create strong connections between people, not stating facts or giving advice."

"What happened with your mother-in-law?"

"The surgery was a success, and she's completely out of the woods. Thanks for asking. She comes home Monday."

Gayle's shoulders relaxed, and she heaved a sigh of relief.

"You know, it's like Nina and Annie. What it all turned out to be was Annie didn't LIKE her new purple sandals in the cubbyhole. She liked her sandals so much, that she wanted them on display. She wanted them on her bookshelf where everyone who came in her room could see her beautiful new sandals with the sparkles on them. But Nina didn't take that into account—those feelings—when she designed her organizational system for Annie's room, and she didn't stop to ask, either. And believe me, Nina is a great mom. This is something we ALL do. All the time."

"If only the entire world could embrace this way of life."

"We could. It's in us; we just don't let it out. Watching children should give you confidence in the transformative power of Total Empathy. Ask Annie to tell you what she's doing with those clams."

Gayle and Bill moved back towards Annie, and Gayle was curious to find her talking to the clams.

"It's time to be free now," she whispered. "Bye-bye . . . " and she tossed them back into the sea.

"All your hard work? You're just tossing them back?"

Annie nodded. "I love the beach. I don't want to take anything away from it."

She went back to digging for clams. "Can you imagine," Bill said, "if we all were determined to leave the world a bit better or, at the very least, to not harm it? To come into a work environment and not destroy another soul for the sake of money or status? We start out that way. We really do. If Sandbox Wisdom becomes a movement, it will change the way the world does business."

"And what if it doesn't?"

"What do you mean? What if it doesn't *catch on*?"

"Yeah."

"Simple. Then *your* workplace and every person *you* come in contact with will be transformed. And that's not a bad start, Gayle, not at all."

"I like this concept a lot. Maybe because I'm a woman, it resonates with my sympathetic side."

"Maybe, but there's another point I have to make. Total Empathy is NOT the same as being sympathetic. Sympathy is merely an emotional reaction to another's suffering. A sharing of feelings. Empathy is more detached and objective, with the ultimate goal being to fully understand without bias or judgment, and then to be genuinely enthusiastic about helping the other person. It requires thinking, as well as feeling. *Total* Empathy means one is compelled to help . . . to make a difference. It's your passion. It motivates you! How can we do this in the corporate world, which is just a microcosm of this one? Well . . . we can start by helping our customers and future customers by making fundamental changes to how we do business. For example, don't *sell* them what you want them to buy. *Help* them get what they want, what they desire. Discover their hopes and dreams. Design products and processes to eliminate customer problems, frustration, stress. Design to engage positive feelings. Create a workplace that respects feelings. Create an environment where people are respected and trusted. Design a business process that places others *feelings* at the center of all you do."

"I know what you mean, now, I think."

"Do you? Fully? Gayle, every single business decision and each interaction is an opportunity to enhance positive feelings, and thus build trustworthiness. Your day is *filled* with occasions to perform small acts, which will produce significant, long-term results. That is . . . if you're aware of them.

They continued talking, but then they both heard Annie let out a giant, "OUCH!" The little girl started crying.

"I cut my finger on a shell and saltwater got in it."

Annie cried as Gayle tried to rub the salt off on her clean shirt. "Is that better?"

"A little," Annie said, still whimpering. "I really wanted that shell. It was the prettiest one I found all day. It had purple and pink on the inside. But now I dropped it in the water. And I cut my finger, too." Her lip quivered.

"I understand how you feel, Annie. I was a little girl once and I got a lot of cuts and bumps. Plus . . . you'll find another shell." Gayle hugged her until she was calm, and then Annie began packing up her beach toys.

"You know Gayle, your response to Annie's suffering was one of those automatic, emotional ones. It was great, but you could have gone a step further. You were comforting her because she cut her finger, but did you use your mind's eye to visualize *her* situation? Did you really care that she dropped the shell? That she felt betrayed by the beach, which is so nice, yet is also a place where she could get hurt? Slow down and put Annie's feelings at the center of your thoughts. Make her feel *uniquely* understood. Her story, her heart, her experience. It wasn't just the cut. It was her friend, the beach. And the shell. The pretty pink and purple one."

"Bill, you are very wise."

The sun was beginning to drop below the horizon. The three of them packed up their things and headed toward the boardwalk. Gayle felt at peace. Total Empathy. She would work at it passionately. She could connect with people and change her social landscape with that as her guide. *The corporate revolution Bill spoke of will start the way all*

lasting revolution start—with one individual at a time . . .
with me!

"Hey Gayle?" Bill touched her arm.

"Yes?" She faced him.

"I, the Purple Knight, would like to invite YOU, the Purple
. . . Duchess! to dinner next week. At Armando's. To celebrate.
First of all, we had a great clam-stomping day with the tribe.
We were able to protect the Purple Princess from the evil witch.
And . . . I really appreciate and sense that you are embracing
Sandbox Wisdom, and I feel so inspired by that. It energizes
me to think this concept is spreading. So let's celebrate, and I
also want to hear what you think of all of this. What do you
say?"

"Purple Knight, as Armando's is the best restaurant in town
. . . and it also has the most divine chocolate soufflé for
dessert, you don't have to ask me twice. The Purple Duchess
will gladly accept. Plus, I can't wait to work these principles
this week and tell you what I've learned!"

Gayle got into her car and drove away. She couldn't
explain it, but she was feeling suddenly aware. As if she had
lived her life like Dorothy in *The Wizard of Oz.* One day, the
world had been black and white . . . and the next, it was all there
in Technicolor glory. This was one yellow brick road . . . no
PURPLE brick road, she was more than happy to follow.

GAYLE'S JOURNAL

* Be motivated by kindness. People want to be understood not entertained!

* Understand others' worlds. Get into their shoes. Understand that for them, their shell may be unique and if they "lose" it they may feel devastated. Not everything is replaceable.

* Defuse the troll with real caring and empathy. Total Empathy.

* Embrace play. Like the Purple Princess and the Purple Knight . . . can't work be full of affection and joy?

* Don't give up when stomping clams. The solutions are there, you have to work to find them.

* An honest, caring question or comment, meant with sincerity, spoken with gentleness, will do more than exploding, ranting and raving, or indifference.

CHAPTER SIX

Education is not the filling of a pail,
but the lighting of a fire.

- William Butler Yeats

✳

*B*ill decided he needed a dose of his old friend Falcon, and planned to spend part of Monday at the garage. He drove up around 3:30, and hopped out of his car, smiling to himself. If anyone had told him that he would have found wisdom in a garage . . . and on a playground, he would have told them they were crazy—a year or so ago. Not anymore. Why shouldn't a guru hold court in a garage? Bill headed back to the pristine white building that housed Falcon's workspace.

"Hey Mr. West!" Annie ran over and hugged him. She was dressed in special coveralls Falcon had custom made for her. "Annie" was stitched in purple on the left front chest pocket.

"Hello princess!" Bill got down on one knee to give her a squeeze. "I'm surprised to see you here."

"Mom is at parent-teacher conferences. It was a half-day at school, so I got to come here and help Grandpa."

"Where is he?"

A hand waved from under the hood of a 1927 blue Duesenberg Boattail roadster.

"Hi, Falcon."

"Hey Bill," Falcon replied. He remained engrossed in whatever problem he had under the hood. "Annie?" Falcon held out his hand, palm up. "Can you get me a half-inch, open-end wrench out of the tool chest?"

"Sure!" Annie walked past the perfectly restored car, its body polished to a gleam. She stood in front of the large red tool chest. It dwarfed her in size. Finding the third drawer down, she searched for a half-inch wrench, found it in a jiffy, and brought it over to her grandfather.

"Thanks Annie Bananie." Falcon continued tinkering. "I'll be done in a minute, Bill."

"That's all right. I'm too stunned to talk. How," he turned to face Annie, "could you pick out that half-inch whatchamacallit out of all those tools in that chest? I can't even check my own oil."

Annie shrugged. "I don't know. I feel like I've always known. Can't remember when I learned it."

Falcon pulled his head out from under the hood. Taking a red rag from his back pocket, he wiped his hands and admired the Duesenberg. "What a *beautiful* engine, the Straight 8. Working with it is pure bliss."

"Falcon, you look like a kid who just got the keys to the candy store. Your enthusiasm with that car reminds me of that quote you shared with me."

"Well . . ." Falcon was still smiling from working on his "baby." "It can't be said that I'm not full of . . . *quotes.* So which one was it?"

"The pursuit of truth and beauty is a sphere of activity in which we are permitted to remain children all our lives," Bill leaned against a workbench. "And you, sir, are a giant kid when you're working on one of your cars."

"A wonderful quote. Uttered by one of the greatest big kids of all times. Good ol' Einstein."

"Well, I still want to know how you taught Annie all about tools. I mean, sure I know what a hammer and a wrench are, but put me in front of your toolbox and I'd be lost."

Falcon patted Annie on the shoulder. "With children, we teach and coach in little pieces, encouraging every step of the way. She said she doesn't remember how she learned it, because she really doesn't. We did it little by little over time and with patience, and now she feels like she's always been a grease monkey." He winked at his granddaughter and continued. "We should do the same things at work. We want people to be up and running so fast. To understand their whole job and all its functions. At once. Instantaneously. But, rather than being so quick to point out what people get wrong, we should be praising their small efforts. And then before you know it . . . they're motivated and they achieve things that they probably wouldn't even attempt on their own. They perform their job as if they've always known how to do it. We haven't undermined their confidence by . . . shadowing them and watching for mistakes every step of the way."

"Yeah," said Bill, "but we need people, in this economy, to get with the program quickly, right?"

"Sure. But our focus must be on our people, and not on simply getting things done. Think about children, Bill. We help them find their *own* success instead of trying to rack up our own. We must do the same with our colleagues, customers, partners. Forget about us, focus on them!"

"Grandpa?" Annie looked up.

"Yes, sweetheart?"

"Can I put the tools away? Are we done for the day? Mom says you should be resting more."

"Yes. You can put the tools away," Falcon said softly.

Bill watched as Annie went over to the neatly laid-out mat by the car, and one by one wiped the tools and took them over to the red chest. Each tool had a place, and she found it. She worked quietly, smiling with pride each time she put one away.

"She loves this garage, doesn't she?" Bill asked.

"Almost as much as I do. Maybe it's in her blood. Or it's in all the happy times we've spent here. She doesn't even realize putting those tools away is a chore. It's all fun. It's all in how you parent, how you grandparent, how you lead. For example, kids seldom resist chores if we work with them. You know, 'You wash. I'll dry.' Or, in the case of this garage, 'I'll fix the car, you handle the tools.' I mean, a garage isn't really a typical place for kids. They could get hurt. So I needed Annie to be disciplined about her time here. But it couldn't be 'I expect such and such to be done . . . blah, blah, blah.' She'd tune me out, and rightly so. We all rebel against commands and authority figures. I don't need to tell her every time she comes here to respect the tools and all that. She's an equal here. We work side by side."

"But don't you think maybe Annie is an exception? She is a pretty special kid. You know that . . . you're her Grandpa, after all."

"Sure. But I believe everyone is special, in his or her own way. I never think of people as being 'bad' or 'lazy'. They may simply have ineffective leadership, or need more guidance. I don't have this pessimistic view that what I have with Annie or what I had when I ran my company, couldn't be modeled a million times over. Look at you! You took my principles and worked miracles with your company."

Bill looked unconvinced.

Falcon looked at his friend. "Look. What happens if I do all the work here? Annie feels like a guest. What happens when executives make all the decisions? People feel like hired hands. They don't feel ownership, responsibility, truly a part of something. They don't feel 'needed.' There's no self-esteem, because they haven't been allowed to figure things out, overcome obstacle. Their work has no meaning. They don't truly contribute. That's why kids join a gang. To feel needed, a part of something bigger than they are. A gang in the corporate world is 'us,' the workers vs. 'them,' the management."

"I see where you're coming from now. Annie feels a part of what you do here, so she respects how you keep the garage. And as an integral part of your staff—after all she has the coveralls to prove it—she's going to take pride in putting things back where they belong and being part of the team."

"Sure. We must give people choices and control over their environment, like we do with our children. It makes them feel a part of the process. Most of us want control . . . some form of it. And although most people think communication is the big problem with relationships, it's actually control. People feel *overcontrolled*. Hence, the tendency for everyone to rebel in some way, internally."

"I call it the troll."

"I like that. That ugly little part of us. Nobody is going to tell ME what to do! That's what that part of us thinks. Managers especially have trouble with this. They feel that if they let go just a tiny bit, it will all come crashing down. They oversupervise and then morale goes down. When people are treated like idiots, they behave that way. They don't share information and a sense of responsibility. Letting go of control is harder than you think. You know, I once heard a story . . ."

"I love your stories," Bill smiled.

"Well, a friend of mine, he is a sexton at a church. Keeps the building clean. Has an apartment out back. He lives a quiet life. Polishes the brass rails, mops the marble floors. Keeps that church awfully shiny. If you met him, you'd never guess the trouble that man had been in before he came to that church. He had a breakdown after Vietnam. Came back . . . got into trouble. Developed a drinking problem. Ended up in prison. Anyway, when he got out of prison, he got the job as the sexton through an outreach program. So the priest, from the first day on, just builds up his self-esteem. He shows him how to polish the brass, and let me tell you, he instilled so much pride in my friend. Little by little. Encouraging. Nurturing. Empathizing. And one Sunday he asks the sexton to help him count the poorbox. And then asks him on Monday to take it to the bank. It's all cash, the poorbox.

"So my friend, he looks at the priest and says, 'Father, I can't do that. I was a thief. That's why I was in prison.' The priest says, 'I don't see a thief before me now.' Well, of course the money was safe with this man, and it marked a total turnaround in his life. He became the good man the priest believed he could become. He wanted to live UP to that expectation."

"Touching story."

"True one. But do you also see the message of control?"

Bill furrowed his brow. "Not exactly."

"Well, think of the priest as a manager. If he expected the

bad outcome and walked behind this man never trusting him to live up to expectations, but instead to stoop DOWN to the level others expected, well, then I think my friend would be out on the streets, robbing and drinking. Or he'd be dead. But that priest took him in as a member of the team. The team should own the outcome. The leader is there to be of service. To influence and inspire. To develop other leaders. The team's job is to solve the *leader's* problems. Gives them ownership, pride. Work must be about the people, and not simply about the plans."

Falcon looked tired. "Annie, let's go have a soda break in my office." He motioned for Bill to follow him.

In Falcon's neat and tidy office, he dug into a draw for change for Annie to get a bottled soda. He kept a vintage soda machine out back. "Here, honey. Go get a root beer."

Sitting down in his armchair, Falcon was winded. Taking a deep breath, he lifted a bound journal on the desk. "Know what this is?"

Bill shook his head. "A diary?"

"Nope. It's a quote book. You know all those quotes I spout? I've been collecting them for years. I have a page marked at two I especially like." Falcon turned the book around for Bill to see.

One was by Pablo Casals: "When will we teach our children in school what they are? We should say to each of them: Do you know what you are? You are a marvel. You are unique. In all of the world there is no other child exactly like you. In the millions of years that have passed there has never been another child like you. You may become a Shakespeare, a Michelangelo, a Beethoven. You have the capacity for anything. Yes, you are a marvel. And when you grow up, can you then harm another who, like you is a marvel?"

The other one, marked with a ribbon was by Anatole France: "Do not try to satisfy your vanity by teaching a great many things. Awaken people's curiosity. It is enough to open minds; do not overload them. Put there just a spark. If there is some good inflammable stuff it will catch fire."

"Great quotes, Falcon."

"I knew you would appreciate them. I want you to have this book someday."

"I couldn't," Bill's eyes welled up. Was he imagining it, or did Falcon seem fatalistic for a moment?

"No. I want you to. When I am done with it. Because you understand what it is I'm trying to do. You understand that living these truths every day makes a life of meaning."

"Thanks, Falcon."

"You're very welcome. So, how's it going with Gayle?"

"Better. In fact, I'm taking her out to celebrate on Thursday."

"Good. Celebrate achievements!"

"Exactly. Small achievements. Large ones. Celebrate them all."

Annie returned with her root beer. "Can we do a clapping game?"

"Sure, honey." Falcon replied and turned his armchair to face her.

"Down by the banks of the hanky panky where the bull frogs jump from bank to banky with a hip . . . hop . . . flip . . . flop . . . missed that banky and a went kerplop."

The two of them moved their hands, clapping and slapping and singing at lightning speed. They laughed uproariously and then Falcon got more winded.

"Honey, Grandpa has to rest."

"OK. You've gone kerplop!"

"I guess I have," he said, as the three of them laughed in unison.

Three nights later, Bill and Gayle sat at a spectacular oceanside restaurant. The view from their table was stupendous. An orange sun, round and perfect, slipped behind the horizon, setting the sky ablaze in pink. And then stars settled in and the sky became an almost luminescent purple. Bill ordered a bottle of champagne.

"To your success," he saluted her with a raised champagne flute.

"To Sandbox Wisdom," Gayle returned.

Sipping and then setting down their glasses, Bill asked Gayle, "So, now that you've been living the principles for a short time, can you explain them to me? Aristotle wrote: 'The one exclusive sign of a thorough knowledge is the power of teaching.'"

"Well, I started seeing the lessons interconnect with some other areas in my life. For instance, I studied the martial arts in college. I wasn't one of those graceful girls. Remember? So I took up Aikido. There I felt both graceful and strong. Anyway, I recalled a lesson I was taught by my instructor, and it hit me . . . it reminded me of the troll. It goes like this: A Zen master once said that inside of him there is both a good dog *and* a bad dog. His student asked him which one he sees more often. And the Zen master answered, whichever one I *feed* the most. The troll is the bad dog. It doesn't care about others, about harmony, sharing, etc. It seeks to satisfy itself. It's own hunger. The good dog is our childlike innocence, which is fed with Radical Awareness and Total Empathy. The more we feed it, the more we will reveal the good dog."

"That's great! I'll have to remember that one," Bill said.

A waiter came over and they ordered their dinners. Gayle was pleased the special was a favorite of hers—lobster tails.

After ordering, Gayle continued. "I believe it was Gandhi who once said 'the only devils in the world are those running around in our hearts. That is where the battle should be fought.' I found this was so true everywhere I looked this week. I kept seeing businesses without empathy. And I began to see how deep it runs."

"Tell me about it," Bill said, pleased Gayle was so animated.

"For starters, there was the telemarketer who called during my favorite TV show—in my busy life, it's the only one I get to watch. You know, I have to deal with customer service all week, so I am actually NICE to telemarketers. They're doing a job. I don't hang up on them. So I told the caller that I was busy at that moment, but if he wanted to call back earlier another night, I would listen to what he had to say . . ."

"That's more than anyone I know would do. So what happened?"

"He didn't listen to a thing I said. He was simply

interested in finishing his spiel. He wasn't interested in me
. . . in hearing me, and finally I DID have to hang up. I thought
. . . this is why people feel so intruded on all the time.

"Then later in the week, I had to call the company I bought
my scanner from. There was some kind of problem with it. I
had run the diagnostics, described my problem, and been told
to return it. They'd send me a replacement. Only problem was,
I was kept on hold for 30 minutes, and on *my* dime—no 800
number—and they were all the way on the other coast!"

"Frustrating."

"Yeah, but that's not all. I wanted to buy a certain type of
pen to see if I liked it. I have to keep notes all day long and my
hand gets tired. I know this sounds silly, but I like a certain
kind of 'feel' in a pen."

"Me, too. I got a pen as a gift from my wife a few years
back, and not only is it my 'lucky pen,' but I love how it feels."

"Exactly. So I wanted to try it out. Only I couldn't,
because the store only sold the pen in packs of ten. Now, I don't
need ten pens that I might not like. But I couldn't buy it in a
single pack. Or even a set of three. Then, when I went to the
drugstore, I simply wanted to buy a tube of toothpaste. I was
packing for a business trip. Have you ever tried to buy a tube
of toothpaste?"

Bill laughed. "You sound like a stand-up comic. Please,
feel free to continue your riff. I don't want to interrupt you."

"Well, not only were there dozens of varieties in all
different formulas, but no two contained the same thing . . . or
bragged about the same thing . . . and no one could explain to
me, on their label, why theirs was best. Nothing was clear-cut.

Imagine . . . being baffled and wasting time . . . and on tooth-paste? I got out to my car and thought . . . these companies must be like chefs who never taste their own food! Are they intentionally trying to confuse me? Do they not care that I don't need ten pens? Do they not know how to keep enough staff on hand so I don't have to be on the phone for a half hour? Do they not know courtesy would be to take my name and number and call me back and not keep me waiting?"

"They lack a little empathy, huh? I'm amused because I see how you're reacting. When I got into this concept, I could look around and realize that my company wasn't doomed. Far from it. If we could operate with empathy, we'd have it over ALL of our competitors."

"Exactly. Listen to this! My brother recently stayed at a really nice hotel on a business trip. He arrived on a Sunday night to find that he had forgotten his dress shirt, and with all the stores closed, he was sure he was sunk. He had a very important business meeting early the next morning. Luckily for him, the bar manager at the hotel, upon hearing Brian's predicament, and without even being asked, called his fiancée and had her bring him a freshly pressed white dress shirt."

"Wow! I'm going to tell that one at my next company meeting."

"Exactly. So will my brother ever stay anywhere else? For heaven's sake, if that bar manager ever wanted to get out of the hotel business and into sales, I bet my brother would give him a job on the spot. That guy, that manager, inherently 'gets it.'"

"And what about your own department?"

"I decided that I needed an empathy check. It's not calls

per hour or profitability per customer, but how knowledgeable and caring our people are that counts. How convenient are we to do business with? How does my department work with internal and external customers? How are we going the extra mile? How are we making a GAME of it, so that we are all having a ball devising ways to be empathetic, to anticipate needs. To have each day be a blast, because we're a team and we're getting it! We're really getting it."

Bill smiled. He lifted his glass again, as their salads arrived. "Bravo! You are, indeed, getting it."

"When I first met with you, I thought this was about how to make my department run more efficiently. Be more profitable. But Sandbox Wisdom seems to be a way of thinking; one that suggests that business is a vehicle to contribute, to enrich the lives of others. To make meaning, and not to simply make a buck. And the wisdom doesn't come from management training or a course in positive thinking. Rather it comes from watching beautiful children like Annie, and the insights and self-knowledge gained by practicing the four principles. It isn't a program aimed at specific metrics. It's about culture change, which is a never-ending journey."

"I think you've got it, Gayle. And I loved the way you explained it. Look at how you described your understanding of the principles. Your brother, the pens, your personal stories. You could have simply rattled off a description of the concepts. You know . . . like a bulleted PowerPoint presentation. But you didn't."

"Out of place in a venue like this," Gayle winked.

"Yes, but really think about it. You couldn't have done anything as instructional or inspiring as what you did with me. Your stories created a sense of intimacy, shared values, trust! Gayle, stories inspire and engage people. They give people something to brag about to their family and friends. Makes their company, and themselves, heroes!"

"I see that now."

"I have a story for you."

"I'm all ears."

Over dinner, Bill told Gayle about his lone major failure in business. It had pained him for years, though with Sandbox Wisdom in the last year or so, he had clarity about how and why it happened. He said he had had a "vision collision" with his former business partners. But instead of dealing with the situation honestly, he had tried to control it.

"I was sure that my partners would never understand the complexity of our business issues. I had convinced myself that these uninformed, passive investors would *react* to the straight truth, rather than help strategically manage the necessary corporate changes. So I hid the truth. I disguised it. And the results were dreadful."

"I'm so sorry."

"It haunted me. Not only was money lost, but I had friendships among my investors. People who had believed in me and my vision—and they were hurt that I hadn't trusted them enough with the big picture. I've learned a lot since—or because of—that experience. I was, as my kid brother put it, a 'Bozo.'"

Gayle laughed. "A Bozo? That's a unique take on it."

"Well, I think he was kind of right. I can really laugh at my mistake now, because I did learn from it. It provided me with lessons that will last me forever. And one of the most important lessons I learned is the need for complete honesty in all of ones relationships. What I refer to as Childlike Honesty. And that will be our lesson for Saturday."

"Can't wait, Bill."

As Gayle drove home later that night, she thought of how Bill had shared both his sense of humor with her *and* his failure—but she truly admired how he had turned it around into something positive. She was, she realized, more sure every day that he was a mentor who was right for her. She was also surer every day that Sandbox Wisdom was becoming a part of her . . . that she would not be able to go back to how she was before. Like the sunset earlier . . . her stars were rising in a new sky.

GAYLE'S JOURNAL

* Failure is all in how you look at it.

* Like an "apple a day," an empathy checkup performed every day will keep my department running smoothly and happily. More than that, we'll transform and excel!

* Find a way to make Total Empathy EXCITING!!! Let my team know that if we come together as a team and seek to transform our department and our lives, going to work every day will be child's play!

* People will rise or fall to meet our expectations.

* Profit is necessary for growth and survival, just like food is. However, it must NOT be our reason for being. What about time and attention to our customers and associates? The emotional connection is the key to our transformation.

* Don't be afraid to laugh at yourself, you Bozo!

CHAPTER SEVEN

*Lying is done with words
and also with silence.*

- Adrienne Rich

✳

nnie and Gayle waited at the entrance to the aquarium. Bill was late, and Gayle looked at her watch, hoping he would arrive in time for the show. As she turned back to face Annie, she saw him dashing across the parking lot.

Doing her best to muster a mock-serious look, Gayle jokingly chided Bill. "Excuse me, Bill, but . . . aren't you a little late? Where's your 'honor'?"

He laughed. "Hello, Ladies. And my apologies for being late. Can you believe I misplaced the tickets? I so wanted us to see the dolphin show and . . . anyway, they were on top of my dresser."

"Well, I for one, am very excited," said Gayle.

"Me, too!" said Annie, the anticipation on her face very clear.

"Well then let's go!" Bill said, and led the way to the ticket-taker.

While waiting in line, Bill glanced at his watch several times. "Hmmm. That's odd. The show was supposed to start ten minutes ago."

"I'm so tired of waiting. When can we go in?" Annie asked.

Bill knelt down. "I don't know, honey. I wish I did, but I don't have an answer right now. Let's wait a few more minutes, OK?"

"OK," Annie sighed.

Annie wasn't the only frustrated child.

"Collective whining seems to be the day's activity," Gayle mused, smiling. "Poor kids. I wonder what's going on in there."

Two minutes later, an employee from the aquarium emerged from a set of double doors. Looking at the faces of several children and then smiling at the crowd, she said, "I'm so sorry to keep you folks waiting, but I have some exciting news. I've just come from our birthing tank where two little dolphin babies were just born."

Everyone in the crowd spontaneously applauded.

"In another minute, we'll let you in and start the show. I know how excited you all must be to learn about our wonderful fellow mammals, the dolphins."

"Did you hear that?" Annie smiled. "Babies!"

Bill leaned over to Gayle. "You know the show being ten minutes late isn't the real problem here. It's the children's— and as a result, the parent's—lack of patience. It's the same with lines at banks, in traffic, on Web sites. The issue is NOT the *time* we must wait. It's our perception. We've been conditioned to expect immediate gratification."

"Don't I know it," said Gayle. "We're always searching for ways to speed things up for *our* customers."

"That's great, but remember to also deal with their perception . . . their emotions. Give them something to do while they wait. Entertain them. Keep them mentally engaged. And for goodness sakes, make sure not to let your customers see— or imagine—your people doing other tasks, when your primary concern should be them. Right?"

"Right."

"It's all about their *feelings*. But instead, what do we do? We measure, measure, measure to death. And from *our* point of view. Things like response time, queue size, etc. Instead, we should be acutely and strategically aware of their *inner* journey with us. You know, give their troll control over the situation. Give them information. Give them choice. Put yourself in *their* shoes, Gayle! Their troll shoes."

"I got ya, Bill," Gayle smiled.

The doors opened again, and Annie pulled Bill and Gayle along and found them seats in the front row of the amphitheater.

"We might get wet sitting here," said Gayle.

"That's the whole idea," smiled Annie.

Soon, a trainer in a wet suit emerged from behind a special rock formation.

"Hello!" He waved.

"Hello!" shouted back a chorus of children's and adult voices.

"Ready to learn about dolphins?"

"Yes!" came back the chorus.

The trainer reached into a bucket and held out a fish. He signaled with his hand and a whistle and a beautiful bottlenose dolphin leapt through the water, did a back flip, and then collected the fish from the trainer's hand.

"Here are some amazing facts about our dolphin, Sheena, here. She has a brain second in size only to humans—you and me. And she has a sophisticated sonar system and an amazing memory."

He reached into his bucket for another fish and threw it into the air where it was retrieved mid-flight by a larger dolphin.

"That was Albert. We named him after Albert Einstein, because dolphins are considered the geniuses of the sea. Dolphins are so smart, I sometimes think they may be smarter than we are at certain things . . . and you know what else? New research has determined that, like us, they are self-aware! They also have the ability to grasp the thoughts of others. Now, we usually think that only humans and great apes can do this. Apes seem to know when their trainers are sad. But dolphins read moods and thoughts, too. Bottom line . . . Sheena and Albert and all their dolphin friends are amazing, and—like most people I know—can't be completely figured out."

"Amazing," murmured Gayle.

Bill nodded. The trainer continued, "My name is Nick, and now we're going to see an amazing film about dolphins. Watch up on the big monitor there, and listen to their communications."

Up on the screen, two dolphins appeared to speak to each other with their interesting clicks, whistles, and voices. Lights flashed, and music played. The children—and adults—were rapt with attention.

Bill leaned over to Gayle, "I haven't seen this particular show before. I am always impressed by how they keep the learning fresh and exciting."

"I think I want a pet dolphin," Gayle smiled.

When the film finished, Nick emerged again. "Time for Albert to show you another trick." Nick tossed rings into the pool and Albert retrieved them and collected his obligatory fish.

"Now," said Nick. "We like to change this show every few months, and change our training routines, too. Think about how you would feel being in a tank all day long. Could get boring. So we like to keep things exciting. And . . .," the trainer gestured, "despite the buckets of fish around the pool, the dolphins DO NOT perform just for food. Albert isn't hungry. The rewards grow out of our whole relationship. My job is to find out what Albert and Sheena and the other dolphins want. It might be a toy, or it might be some ice, or a play session or a rubdown. But training works best if I'm playful . . . it's about our bond. Our friendship. Albert is my friend."

"Ring any bells?" Bill asked Gayle.

"Hmm?" she looked at him.

"It's like our people at work. They learn better if we make things exciting and fun. If we get to know them as individuals, and reward them based on what each person uniquely responds to. We don't simply work for a paycheck and benefits. Just like we don't live to eat. It's about our culture, our relationships, our overall quality of life."

Nick looked out at the audience. "How about a volunteer?"

Children's hands shot up. More than a few adult hands shot up, too. "How about that adorable little girl with the braids?" The trainer pointed at Annie. She glanced at Bill, who nodded, and then she bounded over to the special door leading to the stage. Nick kneeled down to Annie's level and put the microphone up to her face. "So, what's your name?"

"Annie."

"What a beautiful name. How about a big hand for Annie?" The audience cheered. The trainer continued, "And where are you from, Annie?"

Annie turned slightly and pointed to where Bill and Gayle were seated, "The front row." The audience laughed, and Annie smiled along with them.

"Okay Annie-from-the-front-row, let's go over and see the dolphin. Okay?"

He whistled for Albert, who came close to the stage. Nick picked up a bucket of small fish. "Do you know what kind of fish these are, Annie?"

Annie shrugged, "Dead ones?"

As the audience laughed, and Gayle wiped tears of laughter from her eyes, Bill said, "Annie's spontaneous responses are straight from the heart. It's her authentic self. That's what attracts us to her. All eyes are on Annie, but she isn't worried about what others might think. Whether her answers are right or wrong or appropriate. They go straight from her heart to her head, without first being evaluated by her troll. Because with Annie, there is no troll under the bridge. She's present, in the moment with her feelings."

"That's our girl," Gayle smiled.

Nick leaned close to Annie, "Would you like to pet Albert?" She nodded. Nick motioned to Albert, "Come here, buddy."

Annie knelt down by the side of the pool and patted the dolphin's smooth, hard and shiny back.

"What does Albert feel like to you?"

Annie continued to lovingly look down and stroke the dolphin. She finally looked up and with quiet joy in her voice replied, "A dolphin."

"Awww," murmured the audience at her sweetness.

"Bill?" Gayle asked, "People love that kind of honest, candid talk when it comes from the mouth of babes. But not from adults, and certainly not at work. Don't you think?"

Bill shook his head. "The truth today, in this chaotic, fickle business environment, is that we're all pretty skeptical. No one is going to fool or control us! So, we have little tolerance for unquestioned authority. Our radar is always up. Candor, like Annie's, cuts through the radar and creates trust. And trust is the basis of all relationships."

"Makes sense, I guess."

"Let me tell you something amusing, yet enlightening, that happened to me just last month. I was giving a speech at a major conference, and the night before the event, during the cocktail reception, an executive had a large corporate display set up and was giving away T-shirts. I decided to grab a few for my niece and nephew, but upon examination, I noticed that there were no small shirts. I asked the guy, this big-shot executive, 'Can I get a couple of smalls? These are all large and extra large.' The executive looked me in the eyes, noticed my nametag, smiled a big genuine smile, winked and replied: 'Don't worry, Bill. Grab a few for the kids. Those T-shirts are crap. They'll shrink down to a small.'"

"Too funny."

"Exactly, how could you *not* like and trust someone who can blurt out the whole truth, warts and all?"

"I guess that's like a breath of fresh air."

"Sure. People crave authenticity in communication. They're sick of sales pitches, and corporate-speak and euphemisms like rightsizing and restructuring."

"So we need Childlike Honesty."

"Now, more than ever. But let me tell you what is NOT Childlike Honesty. When my bank says they want to be my friend—through expensive ads and promotion—but they still chain the pens down to the counter."

Gayle chuckled. "I never thought about that, though I hate

those darn chained pens."

"But a mixed message. Lacks a certain integrity. For me, Gayle, integrity is all about being you, being real, at ease. Like Annie! It puts others at ease. And it relieves the internal tension that comes from not speaking and being who you really are. It lifts a load and gives you energy! The bank needs to speak to me on that level. Not say one thing and do the other."

"It's the same with fake smiles and phony ads."

"Exactly. Authenticity creates trust, and trust helps create strong relationships."

"With our employees, as well as customers, I'd imagine.

"Absolutely. Trust is required for people to part with their money and share their insights, but it's also required for an enjoyable and innovative work environment. And it's created primarily by people communicating in a straight and honest way."

"Like our Annie. Say what you feel."

"Exactly. Gayle, I believe it's dishonest to feel a certain way and not communicate your feelings. But we do it all the time, don't we? We suppress our feelings and resist. Drag our feet. Talk negatively. This is the same as lying. If you feel it or think it, then you must find a way to communicate it. Because unspoken resistance wastes a lot of time, and drains an organization of its passion, energy, and excitement. Say what you feel has been unspoken!"

"Yes, but . . . " Gayle looked thoughtful. "It's kind of risky, don't you think?"

"Far from it. If we practice Childlike Honesty over time, our credibility increases significantly. People trust us, because we've shown them that we *feel* what they feel. *Think* what they think. We're more . . . human. Imperfect, like them. We have fears, we make mistakes."

"Again, like Annie. Being a little imperfect is an endearing quality."

"Exactly, Gayle. The infallible instinct of childhood. It's about not being afraid to be wrong, or to ask for clarification. Instead, what do most of us do? We make assumptions. Then DEFEND those assumptions. Never make assumptions about what motivates others, Gayle. And never assume that others understand what motivates you. Others do not see or feel the world the way you do."

"Still, Bill . . . " Gayle paused. "It sounds like it requires a lot of courage."

"Not courage, Gayle . . .caring! Childlike Honesty is a very caring way of being, because it's about taking the first step! Speaking your true feelings. And caring is something we need desperately today, especially in the world of business."

"I am really beginning to feel it, Bill. Each day I see a lack of Total Empathy. And now, I'm equally sure I'll see a lack of Childlike Honesty as well."

"I'm sure you will."

At that, Annie rejoined them.

"I had so much fun. And I was great! I really got Albert to do his trick!"

"Good for you, Annie," Gayle leaned over and hugged her. Annie resumed watching the show. Every time Albert swam past, Annie waved.

Bill smiled. "I love that little girl. She wasn't bragging about working with Albert. She acknowledged herself and she doesn't particularly care what we thought."

"If only we could all communicate with such confidence."

"But the troll takes it away. Gayle . . . " Bill paused and looked straight ahead, as if gathering his thoughts. "We all crave communication. We want to share our thoughts, our lives. But we have that darn troll to deal with. Most people have no idea that it even exists. Practicing Sandbox Wisdom means you acknowledge the troll, especially while speaking."

"How, Bill?"

"Well . . . for one thing, by being conscious of the words we choose. Like using the words 'How come?' instead of 'Why?'" 'Why' is our parents talking to us again. It sounds accusatory. 'How come' is softer."

"Really?"

"Sure. Go ahead . . . try it, Gayle. Ask me about my being late today using both phrases."

"Okay Bill. Why were you late today?" Gayle paused. "That sounds hostile."

"Right . . . even looks hostile. Your brow is all scrunched up. Now try the other way."

"How come you were late today, Bill? That sounds more childlike."

"Sure. Softer. Curious, not judgmental. Same meaning . . . different emotional effect. You see, Gayle, our parents and adults around us over time reinforced the negative. They asked us *WHY* all the time. *Why* did we get a C and not an A? *Why* did we stay out past curfew? *Why* did we make such a mess? And as a result, we have this emotional state—the troll—that determines how we will react to various messages."

"I see. Sort of learned patterns of communication."

"Exactly. There are soft, positive ways and hard, negative

ways to express any message. Choose soft, positive, affirming ones. When kids are learning a new skill, like gymnastics, the instructor tells them it will get *easier*, not that it will get harder. But what do we tell people at work about our new initiatives? Really think about it."

"I'm going to start paying attention to the communication cues I give off. This is really hard. Ooops . . ." Gayle smiled. "I mean . . . it will get *easier*, but this is a lifetime of talking."

"Childlike Honesty takes practice, and it requires the other three sides of the Sandbox as well. For example, honesty without awareness and empathy may be insensitive."

"All the sides go together," Gayle looked thoughtful.

"Right. You have to figure out how *you're* feeling, before you willy-nilly start communicating with others. Are you communicating from your caring, inner child, or is it the fear-driven, insecure troll speaking? Is your honesty judgmental, which is really about you? Or are you speaking from your heart, about *your* feelings? Something that can never be debated by anyone."

"So, I should understand my feelings first, and *then* focus on how other's trolls might react?"

"Absolutely. Do everything to keep it calm. To make it feel good about itself. But Gayle . . . you don't want to *appease* people. You want to empathize and influence them with straight talk. Know how you feel and then communicate that feeling, but in a caring way. Get it?"

"I really like these ideas. Once, you master them, you have to feel so . . . free. That's part of it, isn't it? I mean, I can't tell you how many times in my last relationship I used to think, 'I should have said this,' or 'I should have said that.' This isn't just about business. It's about life. Sandbox Wisdom is about the whole package."

"Exactly. It avoids all of those 'should have' feelings. It eliminates the stress of feeling two-faced. How often are things said in meetings and everyone knows it's not true? But we remain silent anyway. When we fail to say how we feel, we by default, communicate acceptance. Our silence is our approval. This is a very dangerous way to operate, especially in a rapidly changing environment. So we should encourage and celebrate the truth-tellers. Now is the time for direct, straight, respectful talk. Hard reality communicated in a soft, caring way."

Gayle thought for a moment. "Last week, a manager I have a lot of problems with approached me and berated me for a report I did. He didn't pinpoint what was wrong with it. He just hated it all. I appeased him by backpedaling a bit. He appeared to be busy, and I didn't want to bother him. But I should have been straight with him. 'How come you don't like it?' I should have asked him how he would have improved it, instead of guessing."

"Exactly, Gayle. Asking others for what you need from them isn't burdensome. You're actually strengthening the relationship, because it requires you *both* to be giving. But it's critical to be present—aware of how things are—without resistance. Figure out what your inner child is feeling and then speak in a calm, relaxed tone. The ideal state is to completely shut down the troll and focus solely on the other person's needs and on the outcome, not on you. And if people don't respond to you, it simply means that you aren't speaking in a way which engages *their* interests."

"I see . . . so it wasn't about me, my ego. It was about a report that a colleague felt wasn't useful to him. Instead, of focusing on his feelings, I got defensive. I kind of resented his non-specific criticism, and worse, I have no way of knowing how to avoid the problem next time."

"That's the key to Sandbox Wisdom, Gayle. Understanding that feelings are everywhere, so you must always be aware and be gentle. That other manager has feelings, even if he wasn't expressing them as anything more than some slightly veiled hostility."

Gayle appeared disheartened.

Bill patted her shoulder. "Don't get down on yourself, Gayle. Old habits die hard. It takes a lot of time and patience to create heartfelt connections. When you expose your authentic self through Childlike Honesty, though, you won't have to defend yourself or ever pretend that you are better or worse than anyone else. You are simply you. Just trust your inner child, and then you'll always know what to say and do."

"Can I bring Childlike Honesty into my workplace? It sounds too good to be true."

"In my company, it's there. We're more candid with each other about our feelings. Therefore, there's less guessing, less rumor. People's feelings are never an imposition on our time. Gayle, leadership requires promoting open and honest communication, especially when times are tough. Because, the troll wants information and control. But, you must all agree to speak with Childlike Honesty at the table. If you don't say it during open discussions, you can't say it behind closed doors later. You must get on board, even if you may disagree. This is the essence of teamwork! A team's decision is your decision. Represent it that way, or get off! These are new models of behavior, which return big benefits over time."

"This seems so revolutionary."

"It *is* revolutionary! Corporations have evolved into a land of innuendo and the 'rumor mill.' It's time to rid the workplace of the B.S.. It's counterproductive to both profit and job satisfaction. When my company's climate changed, we changed. Literally. Our relationships and profits soared. It's real. It happens."

"Oh . . . to eliminate the B.S in my department. I feel like this is a fairy tale."

"Simply start, Gayle. Take the time to see your colleagues as people. Don't tell them what you think they want to hear. Instead, speak from your heart. People can smell a phony a mile away. Play it straight. No hidden agendas. If you have some selfish goals, let them know. Tell the truth. It's captivating. It creates a confident, happy group."

"But, Bill. What if the recession fears or layoff rumors overwhelm *me*? Do I tell my team how I feel then?"

"Do you think there is anything they can do to help?"

"No. Not really."

"Then don't tell them. It will only instill fear, instead of confidence. Robert Louis Stevenson wrote: 'Keep your fears to yourself, but share your courage with others.' Gayle, positive thinking is a great strategy when there is nothing that can be done to change a situation. When the future is unknown and you've done everything you can to influence it, simply tell yourself a story with a positive outcome. Hell, your guess is as good as anyone's . . . so don't worry. Otherwise, you'll appear afraid or desperate, and your influence will go down."

He looked at the dolphin show. The ocean, the marine life, always gave him such clarity.

"I need to add something about fear that Falcon helped me recognize. When we feel doubt, like with a client or manager, what do most of us do? We speed up our talk. Our insecure troll takes over and we try to convince or persuade. Instead, we should slow down. Be gentle and serene, like Falcon, and say what's *really* on our mind. You know, 'I think that we might have a problem' or 'I'm confused . . . so what do YOU think we should do?' Don't ignore your inner voice. If you truly care about the welfare of others, you'll be fearless, Gayle. The troll won't care about itself."

"I won't worry about being rejected?"

"Absolutely not. It's all about intentions. If you're trying to help . . . if it's about the *other* person's interests, *you* have nothing to lose. Think about our world today, Gayle. We're inundated with choice. If we can feel better with a different product, company, person, we'll switch. So, our customers and our colleagues *will* leave us when things appear better for them. But, they'll take their time and they won't think twice about disappointing or inconveniencing us. We mustn't take this personally. It's just the nature of this chaotic drama. But we don't have to be victims. Simply explain how you feel and ask the question, so your time and energy won't be wasted. Make sense?"

"My job, then, is to be truthful? To be myself?"

"Right. And when you say exactly how you feel, without defensiveness or judgment or attacking or accusing, it ends all power struggles and arguments driven by the troll's need to control. Real power is achieved when you stop playing games and roles to get your ego needs met. Why? Because you have all your energy and skills, and it doesn't matter to you if you get rejected. You are not trying to achieve. You're trying to help. You are motivated by kindness. Nothing can stop you!"

Bill then laughed to himself. "You're going to hate this, Gayle, but I have to bring up being on time again. I was late once. So were you. We're all a little guilty of it. People say they keep their word, but they're constantly breaking promises. Living with Childlike Honesty means keeping your word. Appointments kept. Meetings on time. Commitments honored. This creates trust and respect. I try to live it. I know you do, too. But we must always strive to set the best example possible where that's concerned."

The show was soon over and the audience applauded wildly. Annie ran over to the tank to say good-bye to Albert and Sheena.

"I love you, Albert." She blew the dolphin a kiss. Albert swam over to where she was at the glass.

"Do you think he remembers her from the show," Gayle whispered.

Bill nodded. "I do. They connected. Childlike Honesty is a universal truth. It's bigger than us all."

Gayle smiled. Layer by layer, day by day, she was shedding her old ways for something that felt downright revolutionary. She felt so peaceful, playful, and free . . . like a dolphin on the open seas.

GAYLE'S JOURNAL

* Honesty . . . Childlike Honesty . . . if practiced with Radical Awareness and Total Empathy can revolutionize my workplace and my life.

* Childlike Honesty means taking my time to figure out what I feel in my heart. And truly listening to others, making no assumptions about their motivations. And speaking without trying to control or steer the conversation.

* The rumor mill is destructive. Shut it down by promoting open, honest communication.

* People think that an honest expression of our feelings would disrupt order. It wouldn't. It would contribute to it by eliminating passive resistance, wasted time, guessing, etc.

* Make sure people speak freely—even dissent—in meetings. Don't tolerate parroting the party line. This is why people think meetings are such a waste of time.

* People take talking for granted. Childlike Honesty must be taught and encouraged.

* Simply start practicing Childlike Honesty. Maybe this is the way that everything that really matters begins. No guarantees. Just a choice. And hope.

CHAPTER EIGHT

*You can't stop the waves
but you can learn to surf.*

- Swami Satchidananda

ill, Annie, and Gayle met down by the seashore.

"Come on, Bill, aren't you going to tell us what we're doing today?" Gayle asked.

"Top secret," Bill said playfully.

"How about a hint?" Annie asked.

"All right . . . a hint. Well . . . we're meeting someone very special to me."

"Grandpa?" asked Annie.

"No," said Bill. "Not Grandpa. Just wait and see." He looked down at Annie's outfit. She had on orange socks, purple leggings, and a red shirt with hearts all over it. Green ribbons were in her hair.

"That's a pretty colorful outfit, Annie."

"Thank you," she said, proudly. "Yesterday was 'clash' day at school. It was so much fun that Mom said I could dress like this all weekend."

"Good for you!" Bill laughed.

As they walked along, Annie darted ahead, scouting for shells and small crabs and other sea creatures. The smell of the ocean enveloped them. A chill hung in the air, but it was somehow exhilarating. Bill felt so at peace. He listened to the surf lapping against the shore and looked up at the overcast sky. Even a gray day at the ocean somehow comforted him.

"I love it here," he said softly.

"Me, too," echoed Gayle.

"Before we get to the fourth side of Sandbox Wisdom, I want to take a minute to discuss the other three sides: Radical Awareness, Total Empathy and Childlike Honesty. You know, they're very simple concepts, Gayle, but they are *not* easy to master. You must practice them with skill and discipline."

Gayle didn't respond, and Bill spoke again.

"Now normally, when we hear *discipline*, what do we immediately conjure up? Something difficult or negative. But in the Sandbox, it doesn't have to be unpleasant. You'll learn that today as we experience the *fourth* side."

She smiled at him. "I can't wait. Each side of the Sandbox has made my life richer, so far."

"They will, but not without practice. Think about your oil painting. You had to learn the skills and discipline of the painter. You didn't wake up and decide 'I want to paint' and instantly master the craft. And it's the same with relationships. But with relationships, change requires us to learn new skills. The old skills may not be appropriate for today's competitive environment. And it takes time and patience to teach our people these new skills, so that they have complete ownership and are internally motivated to practice them."

"If you had seen my first oil painting," Gayle laughed. "My apples looked like rubber balls."

Bill smiled, keeping an eye on Annie as she jumped from sand dune to sand dune. He continued, "Think about riding a bike. Teaching a child like Annie to ride. We run next to our children, all the time letting them know not to be afraid. That we're always there, next to them, to catch them *when* they fall.

This allows them to soar. But after a while, we don't have to hold on. They can do it! The same with our people at work. Once they have the proper training *and* discipline, we can let go and accept change, knowing that we can rely on *their* skills to make it happen."

They came to the harbor. Bill pointed to some very large sailboats docked at the far end. "Most companies buy this idea of change and patience like they buy a huge sailboat. Once they get it—through a book or a seminar—they keep it docked in the bay and have parties on it on weekends. They never leave the dock because they discover, having bought it, that the disciplines of sailing are difficult to learn and take a lot of time. Instead, they're simply interested in showing it off to others, like business leaders showing off some new program. It becomes a status symbol. Instead, the pleasure should be in doing it. Learning a new skill can be a lot of fun and very rewarding."

The three of them finally arrived to find a small group of people singing, telling jokes, and generally carrying on, while polishing a 23-foot racing sailboat.

"That looks like hard work," Gayle said.

Annie looked up at them. "No . . . they're having FUN!"

"Actually," Bill said, "You're both right!"

Approaching the boat, Bill spotted a laughing face wearing a baseball cap, sitting on the opposite side of the boat. "Oh Captain! . . . my Captain!" he shouted in a playful voice. Those on the boat turned and began shouting hello's in return.

"If it isn't the celebrity CEO!" joked one man in faded jeans and a Harley shirt. "Didn't I see your mug on the front page of the business section last week."

"Hey Bill," said another friendly face.

The captain in the ball cap smiled and said, "You guys are really driving me crazy today!"

A woman in a bright yellow T-shirt joked back, "Hey, Ted . . . I hope it's a *short* drive."

The captain rolled his eyes playfully. Then yelled out, "Hey big brother! Who you got with you there?" His eyes twinkled with obvious pleasure at seeing Bill. He smiled a big grin and swept his arm, "Come on aboard!"

Bill turned slightly to Gayle and Annie as he ushered them to board the boat, "That's my hero . . . my kid brother Ted. Come on . . . I'll introduce you."

Bill offered high-fives to the crew working on the boat as he passed them. "Hi Betsy . . . lookin' good."

Betsy smiled, her gaze looking slightly beyond Bill as she replied: "I wouldn't know, Bill." Then she flashed a broad smile that revealed two engaging dimples.

Gayle realized Betsy was blind. Yet she worked with passion and complete confidence on the beautiful boat. Gayle was amazed and yet not surprised that Bill knew such extraordinary people.

"What's up Hook?" Bill high-fived a burly man with a prosthetic hand.

"Back at ya, Bill," the man joked.

As they boarded the boat, Ted spun his wheelchair around to face his brother. Gayle's sense that something was not quite right was confirmed. She saw that both of Ted's legs were amputated below the knee. Ted and Bill lovingly embraced and patted each other on the back.

"How you doin', Bro? Is this motley crew of yours almost ready?"

"This bunch? We're always ready, Bill. You know . . . " Ted flashed a broad grin and broke into an inspired rhyme. "Here's to it and to it again!"

Ted's crew joined in without missing a beat: "If you get to it and you can't do it, call us, we'll do it. We're used to it, we used to do it, we love to do it, we want to do it, so heeeeere's to it!"

Gayle, Annie, and Bill spontaneously applauded.

"And who are these two lovely ladies with you?"

"This is my friend, Gayle. And this little lady is Annie."

"Wow, Annie, you are one uniquely attired little girl. You're certainly no slave to fashion. Say, are you married?"

Annie giggled, "Noooo."

"Well . . . welcome aboard. I'm the captain of this here crazy crew."

Annie was clearly reading Ted's T-shirt, emblazoned with a beautiful ship and the expression: "A ship in harbor is safe, but that's not what ships are built for."

"What does that mean?"

"My shirt?" He looked down. "It means that if you live life afraid of going on an adventure, then you won't have any adventures. That's not how I want to live. You an adventurer, Annie?"

"You mean, like a pirate?"

"Yeah, kiddo, like a pirate." He smiled at her sincerely and took her hand in his.

"Yes I am. I am Pirate Annie and I'm ready for the high

seas!" She raised an arm as if she had an invisible sword in her hand.

"Good for you, Matey. Well, I've got some things to get ready on our boat here. Want to come with me?"

Annie looked at Bill, who nodded his go-ahead. Annie and Ted headed to the rear of the boat.

Bill walked to the bow of the boat and gazed out over the harbor. Gayle stood next to him.

"Your brother seems very special. So . . . alive!"

"Oh, he is Gayle. And he's also one of the smartest people I know. But not just intellectually, emotionally brilliant as well! Ted has the healthiest approach to life of anyone I've ever met— besides Falcon, of course. He was a Harvard Business School professor and a partner at one of the world's leading consulting firms. He lost his legs a few years ago while saving his two children during a boating accident. Now, he's one of the top disabled sailors in the world, and the captain of this boat and disabled crew, who are preparing for the Paralympic games. He agreed to take us out sailing today and share some of his business insights."

"Wow! I'm honored."

"You know, when he lost his legs, Ted didn't miss a beat. Yeah, he mourned, but he just resolved to keep on facing life the way he always had. He really is my hero, in every sense of the word."

Ted returned with Annie, and they got ready to sail. Gayle admired both brothers' ease with the sails and ropes. The rest of the crew, aboard with them, was equally competent. Their disabilities disappeared as they worked together in a seamless team. They sailed leisurely around the harbor, catching the wind and seeming to skate across the water's surface. Annie gazed in awe as they passed the shoreline in a blur at times, their boat swinging around on a shift in the wind. She wasn't talkative. Just quietly enjoying the wind and the sea, almost respectfully.

"Don't you feel close to the angels out here, Gayle?" Annie asked and held Gayle's hand.

"I suppose I do, Annie," Gayle smiled as a salty breeze blew her hair into her face, and filled her with great peace.

Ted smiled at the two of them. "Gayle. Look at the difference between our sailboat and that big boat out there," his hand pointed to a huge yacht in the distance. "We're able to quickly adapt to changes in our environment, like wind direction and waves. And *this* changing environment is like our changing *business* environment. It's weather that makes the exciting stories in sailing, as well as in business—the upstart winners and the big disasters. And weather in business is simply changing customer and employee preferences, driven by things like technology, innovation, and choice. It took me some to realize this, and to understand that there is really no such thing as loyalty to a corporation or to its products and services. People are loyal to their own feelings . . . period! And it's up to business leaders to keep abreast of these shifting winds and adjust their sails to provide the *feelings* people desire. And do so better than anyone else.

Gayle nodded, but with a puzzled look on her face.

Ted continued, "Gayle, my team always starts our sailing journey with the weather in mind. And every business must start with their customers' feelings in mind. *Experience* what they experience. *Feel* what they feel. Then put in the tools, processes, and technologies to enhance those feelings and extend your lead over time."

"Okay, Ted. But the idea that there is no loyalty . . . I mean, I have brand loyalty. I've been eating the same darn peanut butter since I was Annie's age. My Mom bought it, and even when I was a struggling college student and watching every penny . . . and I could have bought some store brand on sale, I bought *my* peanut butter brand. Now I know that sounds silly, but it's true."

Ted smiled, "You *think* that it's loyalty to the brand, but your peanut butter selection is most likely inertia . . . what marketers call 'habitual buying' or 'cognitive lock-in'. The brand triggers some memories, probably of your childhood, the good old days with your Mom, when times were simpler. When you made decision by means of 'Rocks, Paper, and Scissors.' And so, you respond to those feelings and simply reach out for that particular jar. It's like being on autopilot, almost a reflexive choice. We're creatures of habit, Gayle. We have to be. We just don't have the time or energy to evaluate every choice we make in life. And peanut butter isn't a very critical one."

Ted looked at Gayle with laughing eyes and continued. "In some cases, decisions—like what to buy or where to work—have been driven by limited choice. Think of the 'old economy,' Gayle, as being like 'Gilligan's Island.' Mary Ann *chose* Gilligan, because in *her* eyes, the other heterosexual alternatives—the Skipper and the Professor—were less desirable. She wasn't 'loyal' to Gilligan. She simply didn't have any other reasonable options. Limited choice!"

Bill and Gayle laughed in unison. "You may have me, there," Gayle said, shaking her head.

Ted continued. "It's important not to be blinded by fanaticism for your company or brand today, because our 'new economy' is like 'Temptation Island.' If you can imagine it— any shape, size, color, option—you can have it! It may appear that people have committed themselves to your brand, your cause, or your vision, Gayle. But in reality, what they have bound themselves to is a particular course of action that makes them feel good about themselves and their decision. If someone comes along and offers them a more emotionally heightened alternative, they *will* switch."

Bill nodded, "He's right, Gayle. It's definitely human behavior—feelings—that determines which brands get selected."

Ted surveyed his crew and continued, "You know, it's impossible to learn sailing from a 'how to' book. And the same is true with business today. Much of it is being attentive, responsive to situations without thinking about it. You should teach your people how to be aware, to observe. Remember that knowledge doesn't always take the place of observation. People are able to extract complex patterns and information by being aware. It's like the unconscious intelligence of expert sailors." He paused and glanced at Annie, her black braids blowing in the wind. "Or of beautiful children, like Annie there."

Gayle nodded, "Intuitively knowing what to do under different situations. Like riding a bike."

"Exactly. You see Gayle, knowledge isn't power. Having the knowledge *and* the authority to act when it's time to act . . . that's power! So do things like scenario planning—

planning what to do if such and such happens. It's what sailing is all about! And for goodness sakes, Gayle . . . have a good time while doing it, like I do!" Ted laughed and then popped a wheelie and spun his chair in a circle. "My mission is to put the 'fun' back into dysFUNctional!"

Ted smiled at his brother and moved his wheelchair forward to attend to something with the rigging. Bill looked at Ted fondly, then shifted his attention to Gayle. "He epitomizes the fourth principle of Sandbox Wisdom . . . Enlightened Humor. A light-hearted personality. Someone who takes his passion for people and sailing seriously, but not himself. Ted realizes that we're all more alike than different. That we're all just little waves in the vast ocean of life. He's always lived with humility, understanding that he's NOT in control. Ted says that stardust blinds more people than sand, so he has never let his various achievements in life give him an inflated sense of self. No arrogance. He truly is a person of spirit. Like Falcon, he is cheerfully carefree."

"He's wonderful," Gayle replied with a smile.

Bill watched the crew maneuvering the boat. "They all are. Such a passionate, fun-loving bunch. You know, a sailing team is what you make it. And a business, a department, is also what you make it. You can either make it a machine—unemotional precision, robot-like. Or enjoyable, a community. Why is it that children—like Annie—are the only ones who believe that life should be about sharing and fun?"

"I don't know. I guess we all grow up thinking that we should face responsibility head on and seriously."

"We were programmed to think that way, Gayle. But it's an erroneous way to perceive life, more today than ever. The world is a very chaotic place. A complex, web of interrelated conditions and relationships. There are no absolutes anymore. But when setbacks occur, as they inevitably will, we *still* seem to focus on just a few possible causes . . . the ones that relate to us! As if everything that happens *to* us is *because* of us. This is our egocentric nature again. Our troll. We filter the world through it. And it fills us with frustration, anxiety, worry. It destroys our peace of mind. We must drop this view, and instead of reacting, be humble and patient. Laugh at the setbacks. That's what Enlightened Humor is all about. Understanding that we are NOT the center of the Universe. We are NOT in control. We're all in the very same boat . . . searching!"

Gayle took a deep breath and paused for a moment. "You know, this past year has been an especially difficult one for me. The amount of change has been overwhelming at times."

"And there's going to be even *more* adversity and change, especially in business. Contacts that we spent months working with will leave to go to another company. People who promised to call us, or to meet with us, will be sidetracked by something more important to them. But, we must be like a sailor in a storm. Composed. The sailor doesn't identify himself with the conditions. They just are! The same with relationships. You can either let the waves make you sick, like a passenger on a luxury liner. Remain passive, be a whiner. Or see the waves as a source of excitement and fun. Be active, and ride the waves, like a surfer. Have a sense of hope, not despair. Laugh!"

Laughter, I can certainly use more of that in my life, Gayle thought. "I love being out here. It's so relaxing."

Ted rejoined them. "I heard that, Gayle. Glad you're enjoying yourself. It *is* relaxing out here . . . today. If you're at sail with no destination in mind, like we're doing right now, what do you do? You take the easy route. Wander around. That's why an organization needs to provide a sense of purpose, its values, team rules, how it does things! This sets the overall direction. Gives people the freedom to act within certain boundaries, and without being micromanaged . . . which creates trust. It's like a keel on a sailboat. Keeps the boat stable during turbulent times."

Ted quickly looked around to check on his team. "It's about mentoring, not monitoring. Having few rules and procedures, which question the honesty or competency of others. On my boat, it's more important to behave sensibly than follow a chain of command. Stuff happens much too fast while racing—and in business today—for a command-and-control approach to be effective. In extreme conditions, you must make rapid decisions. You want people to create and innovate, not simply take orders and react. You need to tap into their innate wisdom."

"Think on your feet," Gayle nodded."

"I prefer to think on my wheels," Ted joked. "But you're right, Gayle. When you sail, you don't get where you're heading in a straight line. You adjust your course to fit the changing conditions. And you can't always wait to see what the wind will do. For example, it's really dangerous to get into a big wind with too much sail up."

Bill chimed in, "All worthy efforts require course-correction. Like tacking with a sailboat. Get people engaged in the change. It's part of the trip! And they will tolerate near term unknowns, if you get them involved in charting the course and keep everything out in the open. You must learn to work together. There's no time to debate endlessly or argue. Improvise and move forward. You're interested in performance, not appearances."

"Exactly, Bill. But Gayle . . . please remember . . . NEVER deny the wind. Sailors always keep the wind in their sails. They use the wind to their advantage, just like business people should never deny other people's motivations . . . their feelings."

"Use the wind to my advantage." Gayle looked at Annie. "I will, Ted. And I also want to have fun like Annie . . . and like you. Can I do that at work?"

Annie leaned her head against Gayle's arm. "I hope you can, Miss Gayle. I would hate to think you have no fun at work. After last week, I want to be a dolphin trainer when I grow up so I can always have fun. But now . . . maybe I want to be a sailor."

"She's delightful," Ted nodded. "Gayle, the only difference between work and play is attitude. Annie instinctively wants to have fun while she's working. Children are at play in the Universe. We should all train to have their instincts. Rediscover your inner child, Gayle, and become more playful . . . move other people's hearts."

"That's what Falcon taught me," Bill added. "We get so hung up on the outcome, that we don't enjoy the journey. Like with a dog: It's chasing the car that's fun, not catching it!"

Gayle and Annie both laughed at Bill's zany analogy.

Bill laughed with them. "I mean it. Enlightened Humor changes how others interact with you, which then changes you, and vice versa. I tried desperately in the past to reach busy executives by leaving 'traditional' voice mail messages. But with no luck. Instead of getting impatient and bitter, I saw the humor in it all and so, I decided to leave some humorous messages. And you know what? People started returning my calls. Why? Because humor is disarming. Those busy people are ALSO frustrated, tired, feeling a little negative. They want something to make them smile, brighten up their day. You might as well play phone tag with someone who goes out of his or her way to add some cheerfulness to your workday. A light-hearted approach enhances relationships."

Ted nodded. "Enlighten up! Stress builds up over time, and it's costly to any organization or team. It hampers right action, risk-taking, creativity. Humor breaks the stress."

"It's like playing a sport," Bill said. Take tennis. When you're confident and relaxed, you don't think about the ball coming. You're loose. You're not afraid to make great plays."

"Yeah," Gayle chimed in. "It's the same with Aikido."

"Sure," Ted agreed. "It's the same with most sports. People think you must be intense and serious all the time. Humor helps athletes stay calm. You can have fun *and* concentrate at the same time. Heart *and* head. That's what we should all be striving for. Recapture the delight and wisdom of childhood, without losing the advantage that comes from our wonderful intellect."

Annie smiled. She liked being part of Gayle and Bill's special Saturday.

"You have a terrific smile, Annie." Ted smiled back at her. "And you know, Gayle . . . a beautiful smile, like Annie's, is a smile, no matter what language we speak. We can smile a genuine smile whether we are Asian or African-American; whether we are from Montana or Mozambique . . . it doesn't matter. Humor and laughter bind us together more tightly than anything."

"How can I build on that with my team?" Gayle asked Ted.

"Well, first, by demonstrating that you don't take yourself seriously. Your people will FEEL closer to you; they'll want to be around you. You'll be more likable and approachable. Also, with my crew, we have certain rituals we go through. Before a race, we spend time telling stories about past races. We discuss what went right and wrong. We discuss the day's weather, and other things to be aware of. Jack likes to sing sailing songs in his foolish looking Viking hat. We make silly bets. We cultivate a sense of humor AND an appreciation of the absurd."

Ted looked off at the shoreline with wide eyes. "One time we were out on our final practice run before a big, qualifying race. Two guys on our team spotted a pelican caught in an oil slick with some fishing wire in its beak. It was a mess. We managed to capture it, had it below in a tub of water, flapping around. We were all oily, messy . . . and we started laughing so hard that we couldn't stop. Then Charlie made up this ridiculous song about pelicans . . . if he sings it to this day, I fall over laughing . . . it was absurd. But you know, we were closer after that day than after anything we ever did together— and seemingly, it was a wasted session. Yet we learned a lot about each other and our shared values. The Great Pelican Rescue Race, we call it."

Annie clapped her hands. "I'm so glad you did that."

Ted looked her in the eyes, "I am, too, Annie. I really am."

Ted looked upward. The wind had picked up and the sky was slowly darkening. "Gayle, when people tell you to 'grow up', do you know what they're really saying? 'Conform . . . be a good little robot, like me.' Well I say, nonsense! Go with the passion that arises in you heart. Take delight in the moment, like a child. Accept yourself. You're perfect the way you are! Look at me. I accept myself. Good and bad. Like my accident. People ask me all the time if the accident impaired my sailing abilities. You know what I tell them? 'It has actually helped. I don't get cramps in my calves anymore!'"

Gayle and Bill smiled. Ted continued, "I never take myself too seriously. I'm the captain, but I take out the trash, scrub the deck, clean the head."

"And I bet it gets rid of the troll, too!" Gayle whispered to Bill, who nodded.

"Right," said Bill. "And Ted taught me something about my associates that I never fully appreciated. He says that people don't leave ships, they leave skippers. And the same is true with the people at my company, and yours, Gayle. People don't work with *everyone*. They work with a few people, their immediate manager being the most influential. That's you!"

Ted looked up at the clouds again, which seemed to have grown heavier and darker. "I think we might be in for some rain, folks."

Annie piped up, "Do you want to know if it'll rain or not today, Captain?"

"Sure," said Ted. "Are you some kind of fortune teller?"

"Kind of." She pulled a folded-up "cootie catcher" out of her pocket.

"I remember those!" Gayle squealed. "I don't remember how to make one, though. You pick numbers and colors, right?"

Annie nodded, "Yup. Go ahead . . . pick a color."

Gayle looked down at the origami-like contraption stretched tightly across Annie's fingers. "Red," answered Gayle.

"R . . . E . . . D . . . " Annie's fingers manipulated the folded fortune teller. She opened it and looked at Ted. "Pick any number you see in here, Captain."

"Four!"

"One . . . two . . . three . . . four. Okay pick a number again to see the answer."

Bill said, "Three."

Annie opened the fortune behind the flap marked 'three'. "You may rely on it!"

Gayle frowned. "Oh, no . . . rain."

Annie, on the other hand, grinned and yelled, "Hurray!"

Bill looked at Annie's face, staring up at the sky with anticipation. "It's so funny how we adults react to things we can't change, like the weather. Kids love it all. They go with it . . . go outside and jump in puddles. Adults whine and moan and complain. Kids skip down the street. Why don't successful business people skip down Wall Street? It's all about attitude."

Ted looked in his brother's direction. "Sure. When we lose a big account we can yell and scream and point fingers, or we can grab some noisemakers and decide it's time to figure out how we lost them, why we lost them, and then celebrate that we learned something in the process. Yahoo! When we lose a race, we don't turn on each other. The crew grabs a few beers and we figure out what we learned. We bond over it. It's all in the attitude. And then we set our course for the next time, bolder and stronger than the race before."

Rain began to fall in large drops, and Annie caught them on her tongue. Soon, they were drenched, and Annie shivered slightly. Ted rolled over to a storage bench and took out a large yellow rain slicker. He helped Annie into it, then shouted to his crew to head for the dock. After tying the boat up, Bill, Annie, and Gayle each hugged Ted good-bye.

"This was the most memorable day. I can't thank you enough for sharing your boat and your wisdom with me, Ted."

"Any time, Gayle. But next time, you're polishing the boat with the rest of us," he squeezed her hand. "And remember, there are no second-rate jobs, just second-rate attitudes."

"You got it, Captain."

Bill, Annie, and Gayle headed back toward where their day had begun. The showers had stopped, and the beach had a sweet rain scent.

"Smell that?" Annie asked.

"The seaweed?" Gayle asked.

"No . . . the angels again."

Gayle smiled and reached out to hold Annie's hand while she walked along the shore.

Bill smiled and added, "Know why angels fly, Gayle?"

Gayle shrugged and shook her head.

Grinning, he answered, "Because they take themselves lightly."

Gayle nodded slowly and smiled. *It was all in how you looked at it.*

GAYLE'S JOURNAL

* Bill and Ted enlightened me today. If I live in shallow waters, my external environment will stir up the muck in my mind and blur my vision. Then when the situation gets calm again, I'll see clearly. So, I should go deep within. Don't let the stress of my job soak my energy. Have fun! Laugh! Trust myself, my instincts, my inner child. It's always clear there. The turbulence can't get down that deep. I must remain in calm waters.

* Saw a bumper sticker that pretty much summed up the day: "She who laughs . . . lasts!"

* Laugh. At myself. At life. At fear. And NEVER, EVER deny the wind!

CHAPTER NINE

We have no more right to consume happiness without producing it,
than to consume wealth without producing it.

- George Bernard Shaw

*B*ill, and Gayle walked down the beach, shoes in hand,
away from Ted's boat. After the brief rains, the air seemed very
still. Except for a lone gull, the shore was silent. Annie played
in the waves, rushing almost into the water. Then, as the ocean
swelled up the shore, she ran back to drier sand, trying to keep
the ocean from "tagging" her—it was like her own game of
catch. She yelled back to Bill and Gayle, "Did you guys know
that every seventh wave is the biggest one?"

The horizon was a beautiful shade of crimson as the sun
began to set behind it. A warm sweet breeze blew in from the
ocean. Gayle looked around. It seemed that the earlier rains
had chased away all beachcombers except for them. She felt
almost reverential as she and Bill walked in silence, strolling
beside each other for what seemed like an eternity, blissfully
soaking in the magic of the ocean.

Annie's game of catch made Gayle think back to her own
childhood. What Ted and Bill had said to her today made such
total sense. That was a sign of truth, she knew. Her internal
barometer, that measure of reality versus falsehood, told her it
was so. Why did we have to leave a game of catch with the
ocean and all those childhood pleasures and energies behind?

Bill reached down, grabbed a flat stone and flung it into
the ocean. He finally broke the silence: "Well, that's it."

Gayle deep in her thoughts muttered, "Huh?"

"Finis. Fait accompli! That's all she wrote."

"Oh . . . that's right. Our Sandbox lessons are over. It feels sad somehow. The end."

Bill smiled ruefully, "Don't worry. It's never complete; in fact, it's really just beginning. But to celebrate the end of *this* leg of your voyage, Gayle, I have a surprise for you . . . up ahead there."

Gayle looked and saw a small group of people seated around a campfire near the water's edge. Gayle couldn't figure out who they were. Then a tall, lean shadowy figure stood and waved to the trio. Annie recognized the silhouette of the man in an instant and squealed with delight, "Grandpa!"

Breaking into a full sprint, she dashed toward the group and jumped into Falcon's arms. He squeezed her tight and spun her around. As Gayle and Bill approached, they saw Deanna Cunningham—"Mom" from Bill's company, as well as Annie's mother, Nina. In the gathering darkness, introductions were made all around. Stars gathered like crystals in the sky, and the surf sounded as it lapped the shore, but all that was visible were white lace ruffles of water skirting across the surface.

Falcon embraced Gayle, "Well, what do you think of our campfire crew? How are you feeling?"

Gayle laughed, enjoying the embrace of her old friend. "Truthfully? A little overwhelmed."

Bill smiled and put a hand on her shoulder, "In Falcon's usual way, he anticipated that ending our Sandbox sessions might feel overwhelming, but really, they're meant to inspire and focus you. So this final session was his idea. Just hang out at this fire, share and reflect. No specific message. Just sharing."

"That's not true," Falcon interjected.

Bill looked at him, puzzled.

Falcon bent over and pulled out a plastic bag and some sticks. "There are the marshmallows to roast!"

Gayle looked into his eyes. The man radiated peace, depth and knowledge, but also a playful, happy innocence.

"Marshmallows are about as close a food to childhood as you can get!" Falcon added.

"Now Dad," chided Nina, "can you really call them a FOOD? More like a confection. Goo!"

Annie jumped up, "No! They're a food."

Falcon laughed, "OK, so perhaps they're not an obvious member of any food group, but 'enjoyment' should always be part of our day. Otherwise, why get up, why live? The poet Kabir wrote, 'Do you have a body? Don't sit on the porch! Go out and walk in the rain!' And he might have added, 'eat a marshmallow now and then; it's good for your soul!'" And with that, Falcon jumped up and darted towards the ocean. Annie ran after him. They grabbed each other's hands and danced in circles in the water, splashing and laughing, the spray kicking up about them, two shadows playing in the darkness."

Bill mused, "When did we stop being outrageous, like Falcon? When did we stop playing? Stop singing? Stop being fascinated with our journey? When did the brightness leave our eyes? You know, since what we make of our lives is up to us, we can either create a life filled with passion and possibilities, or—like those big boats in the harbor we saw earlier today—stay safe and secure, never experiencing the marshmallows, the surf, the angels at the seashore."

Returning wet and sandy, Falcon handed Annie a warm blanket and they all settled around the campfire. Nina handed Annie a long stick with a marshmallow on the end, and after some instructions on safety near the fire, Annie began to toast her marshmallows.

Falcon spoke to Gayle, Bill, Nina and Deanna. "We're here to help Gayle end her sessions and embark on her own journey in the Sandbox. Remember that for each of us, the Sandbox has our own frame of reference. We can't judge another person's take on what it all means . . . but then again, you are all Sandbox veterans now. You inherently KNOW we don't judge, but instead offer support. I don't have to tell you that. This is the beauty of us all playing in the Sandbox together."

Facing Gayle in the light of the fire, Falcon asked, "So, why are you here, Gayle?"

Gayle looked puzzled: "Why am I here . . . today?

Falcon added, "Why are you here, on earth, at this place, at this time?"

Gayle pondered, then said, "I guess, to do what I do to the best of my abilities and do it in a way that makes the world a better place. And also, to help my team be successful."

Deanna smiled in support, "That's wonderful, Gayle? And *think* about the people you work with. How would you suggest that *they* make the world a better place through *their* work?"

Gayle's brow furrowed, not yet sure how to answer that question. Her mentor, Bill broke in, "That's a very important question, Deanna. Do you mind if I share some of our discussions on the subject with Gayle?"

"Of course not," Deanna replied.

Bill spoke clearly, with great impact, "Work must be meaningful to *everyone*—from CEO to janitor—for a company's values and strategy to be embraced and reinforced daily. And it can be, if we use our work to build bridges between people. To enhance relationships and positive feelings. This, then, makes the *world* a better place."

Falcon nodded, "That's right, Bill. It's all about feelings . . . of respect, appreciation, dignity, control over one's life. When I joined the workforce—as a low-wage laborer, then as an engineer, then manager, and eventually as a CEO—I, as well as most others, had a large support network of family, friends, church group affiliations, even my neighbors. These relationships provided the positive feelings needed to keep us whole and emotionally healthy."

Bill added, "The troll's needs were being met."

"Exactly. But the world is different now. We're all isolated, rich and dissatisfied. There is widespread discontent. Companies today have a unique opportunity to improve this human condition, both for their customers and their associates. And it's a huge competitive advantage for any business, because people are now actively *seeking* these types of relationships. We are starved for these feelings."

Annie, by now, had her fill of marshmallows and was leaning on Nina's arm, blanket wrapped around her, fighting her eyes closing. Falcon smiled at the sight and gently rubbed Annie's head. "And this, in turn, helps improve the world for our young ones."

Nina spoke quietly, to avoid disturbing Annie, "Dad, you are *so* right. When I changed my business philosophy and at that same time focused on providing my people with control over their work and their lives, everything changed. We began to achieve clarity on what's truly important . . . to our customers, as well as to each of us!"

Bill remembered his company's changes, "Saved us a hell of a lot of wasted time and money. Ended all of our assumptions about why people do business with us. We now focus all of our time and energy on what *they* care about. On *their* feelings."

Annie could fight sleep no longer.

"Look at her," Deanna said, "she looks so at peace."

Gayle smiled, "Spending Saturdays with her has been the best adventure. She's such a treasure."

Falcon spread another blanket on the sand and Nina gently laid her daughter down on it, using a balled up jacket for a pillow. She kissed her forehead. "I guess you all wore her out with sailing today."

Deanna laughed, "Wore her out is right. So Gayle, what did you think of Bill's crazy brother, Ted? Now, he's sure full of energy, huh?"

Gayle smiled, "He's wonderful. So smart, and yet so down to earth. I really learned a lot from him today."

Bill tossed another log on the fire, "Anything specific stick out in your mind?"

"Well, the whole idea about the wind in business. That we *can't* direct the wind, but we *can* adjust our sails."

Falcon asked, "Do you think it has always been that way, Gayle? The wind, and all?"

"I suppose it has, Falcon. In the past, people simply didn't have as many options—the pace of change, of innovation in business, was much less. Therefore, customers' preferences

—their changing feelings, the wind—wasn't blowing us around as much."

"Excellent analogy, Gayle!"

Nina sat down again, "Exactly. And these changing feelings, the wind, are the insights we need to stay competitive, to increase profitability. Think about it. If we all have the same information and knowledge, how are any of us going to make any money?"

Falcon slapped his knee, "Wow! Even my little girl gets it. Making others happy not only makes *you* happy—because you feel effective and useful, but it also gives you a competitive advantage in business."

Falcon stood and pushed a marshmallow onto a stick. "Who wants one golden brown?"

Gayle raised her hand, and before long, they were all eating soft, warm and satisfying marshmallows.

"This does take me back . . . to Girl Scout camp." Deanna smiled, "So Gayle, I hear that Ted is one heck of a sailor."

"I don't sail, so it's hard for me to judge. But he appeared to be one outstanding captain. He talked about having everything out in the open with his crew—mistakes, successes. He emphasized that they share knowledge and share responsibility for the fate of their race. And also that they have a passion for racing and for each other. They have rituals; they play and have fun together!

Billed smiled, "Ted understands that the captain must focus the team, channel their energies. He shows them where they need to go . . . what may happen next. He plans with them, not for them. And he is aware that sailing requires quick learning. Like life, there is no perfection in sailing. You must quickly commit to action, even though you can't see the ultimate destination. Because conditions change so frequently, the best we can hope for are appropriate actions and learning—not perfection."

Deanna put her hands up to the fire to warm them, "A great metaphor for business, and other relationships, in this chaotic world."

Falcon sat down again, having had his fill of his favorite sticky treat. "Absolutely. The wind has certainly kicked up and it is swirling. We mustn't tighten up and become inflexible and autocratic. Instead, we must all pay attention and be quick and flexible, able to adapt and change roles like when sailing. But don't forget that relationships take time. They must be nurtured."

Deanna nodded, "You're right, of course. I think many business leaders, in their haste to move forward, forget to focus on building and nurturing relationships. They neglect building shared values and history by taking the time to tell stories, to get to really know each other . . . quality face time."

Bill looked at Gayle, "Falcon certainly taught me the importance of personal contact, and of inclusion. Of feeling a part of something. At my company, we're together on every-thing. We know that we're all connected. We're truly a team. Now . . . we're not equal. We do have different roles, and decisions are made by those in positions to best make them. But once everyone is heard and the decisions are made, it's all for one and one for all."

Falcon said, "Gayle, I've had the great pleasure of meeting Ted as well. What struck you about his character?"

"His sense of wonder and humor, Falcon. The whole idea of Enlightened Humor . . . I never realized the importance of its place in a business environment."

Deanna clapped, "You got it, Girl! We don't need stress-reduction courses at work. We need *troll*-reduction courses. We all need to lighten up!"

The group laughed. Bill patted Gayle's shoulder and said, "Well . . . it's getting late. And I know how much Gayle wants to say her good-byes and get on with her personal Sandbox Wisdom journey—at work and with her personal life."

Nina said, "One more thing everyone. Dad? Before we head our separate ways, do you think you could take just a minute and give us *your* view on all of this. I mean . . . you've been studying this stuff since before any of us were even born. What do ya say?"

Bill nodded, "Come on Falcon."

Falcon was silent, thoughtful. He picked up Annie's hand, soft and tiny, and placed it in his own. He rubbed her cheek as she slept. Looking up at his assembled group of friends and loved ones, he stared each one in the eyes, meaningfully, lovingly, "There's a passage in the bible . . . I think it's Matthew, Chapter 18, Verse 3. It basically says that unless we turn and become like children—like little Annie here, we will never enter the kingdom of heaven. So I have a question for you all to think about. When did we lose our innocence? When—to use Bill and Deanna's metaphor—did the ugly troll come into being, with its desire to compare and control? When did we stop *being*—aware, caring, loving, uniquely *us*, and instead start striving to *become*—powerful, famous, success-ful, somebody!"

No one answered. Their gazes were fixed on the flickering flames of the fire. They were obviously deep in thought.

Falcon ran his hand through Annie's hair and continued, "Our intellect is our problem. Our 'knowledge' prevents us from experiencing with our hearts. We must be more like Annie and explore life without judgment of ourselves, or of others."

He stared off into the darkness up the beach, then into the fire, "Listen . . . I think that the four sides of Sandbox Wisdom are a *perfect* allegory for business, and for life. Like the few sailing skills required to channel the wind, these four sides will allow you to effectively deal with the continuous, ever-changing nature of relationships. But first, you must recognize that the myths underlying our business culture and underlying our common sense have not taught us to focus on people's feelings. On the contrary . . . we've been told to be *tough*, leave our feelings at home, and other nonsense like this. Once you acknowledge this fact and realize that feelings are the *key* to your ultimate success, the rest is relatively simple."

Falcon looked each of them in the eyes again, wanting to be sure to convey his message. He always spoke with great passion, yet he was never aggressive or cynical. "To summarize and paraphrase what Bill has been sharing with Gayle during the past four weeks, we must begin our journey—any journey, really—with awareness. And this awareness must be both internal—an understanding of our mental programming . . . the thinking in our heads . . . and external—an unbiased, fresh look at the world. Remember that society will try to shape your views. But instead of submitting, you must be fearless like the child in the story, 'The Emperor's New Clothes'.

Don't force yourself to believe simply because others do. Rather, see the world with innocent eyes and expose the emperor's nakedness. Also, let's stop trying to bend the world and those in it to meet the selfish, neurotic desires of our troll. It's an impossible task in this ever-changing environment, and it will simply drain you of your inborn passion and carefree nature. So be *radically* aware. Be alert, observe, question, explore. Stop being a robot to your cultural programming. Be a rebel . . . be a child again.

"Second, now that you are free from the voice in your head . . . now that you are in control of the only thing that you can ultimately control—your own thoughts—you will begin to see people and things as they *really* are. I say *really* are, because unless you have silenced your troll, you will continue to see people as your *troll* wants you to. You'll see them as generalities, or you'll see them selectively, as sources of what may threaten or benefit your ego. Instead, see like a child. See each person and thing as what it is. Unique, remarkable! A manifestation of the eternal! Understand, with *total* empathy, that people's conditioned trolls are also controlling them and driving their fears, their desires, their decisions. See the world through *their* troll's eyes. Don't fight with their trolls . . . don't resist them. Calm them. Help them find *their* success. Be understanding, gentle and caring. And let this caring impel you to action."

He kissed Annie's hand and let her curl it up against her again. "The third ingredient . . . is to be nakedly innocent, like Annie. How? By practicing Childlike Honesty. By tuning into—and trusting—your internal signals. By caring enough to be the first to reveal your 'true' feelings to another. By realizing that being a little imperfect is being a *lot* human. By not maintaining a facade, not fearing group pressure. By telling the plain truth, even when it's hard. Children aren't held back by fear of disapproval like we are. We must break out of our mental prison of societal approval. What do you care what other people think anyway? Sure . . . do things for others. But don't do them so that they will *like* you. Stop *manipulating* the moment, and do as Bill suggests—*master* the moment! Trust your beautiful inner child, and you'll know exactly what to say and what to do.

"And finally, remember that life is a mystery to be lived, not a problem to be solved. Live it with passion and a healthy sense of humor. Get over yourself . . . you're not that important! Use humor to cope with the surprises inherent in this chaotic world. A healthy sense of humor gives you the courage you need to push forward to help improve conditions for others." Falcon picked up a handful of sand and let it stream between his fingers.

Nina broke the group's silence. "Dad. Tell them what happened last week with you and Annie at the garage. You know . . . the bump on the head thing?"

Falcon looked down at Annie's peaceful face and laughed quietly to himself. "Last week I was having a moment, trying to repair a friend's beautiful 1923 Ford T-Bucket. I was battling with this foolish rusted nut that wouldn't budge. Anyway, I guess we all slip back now and then, because my frustration got the best of me. I was pulling on the wrench, sweating like mad, with no success. So I jumped up, pissed off, and banged the top of my head on the hood. I lowered my head, pissed off even more, and in frustration, I lifted my head and bumped it *again*!"

Everyone in the group was totally engaged in Falcon's story. Bill laughed, "I guess we all do things like that. I know that I do."

Falcon continued, "Anyway, Annie saw this and she cracked up. 'You are SO funny, Grandpa!' Watching her belly laugh knocked me out of my self-imposed rage. We both ended up on the garage floor laughing. Later, I calmly went back to the task at hand and solved the problem. You see, all that my rage and frustration did was make the problem worse. And it was humor that helped me realize it. Folks . . . life itself is play. Enjoy it. And please remember why you're doing what you do. Success is about who you are and how you act, not what you have. Use your work as a vehicle for building relationships and friendships, and for having fun."

Gayle noticed that Falcon looked spent, tired, as if he had poured all of his energy into making absolutely clear to them the principles of Sandbox Wisdom. She felt grateful that he had decided to introduce her to Bill . . . that all of them now shared a vision of how it could be.

"Thank you so much, Dad," Nina whispered.

"Yes, Falcon. Thank you," Bill echoed. "Well, there you have it from the master, Gayle. Relationships are the new bottom line in business, and this way of thinking—Sandbox Wisdom—is the way. And trust me, you can't fake this stuff. It has to be in you. Part of your being. As someone once said: 'It's the person who likes to pat dogs to whom dogs come for pats.' The same is true with customers and our colleagues. And don't think that this way of thinking takes a lot of time. Ways of being, habits, take a lot of time to break. But a way of thinking—this transformation—only takes a second. It's a shift in perspective. It's being a child again."

Gayle looked around at the group. She suddenly felt genuine tears stinging her eyes. Yet, because of Sandbox Wisdom, she wasn't afraid of them. She allowed one to trail down her face. "Thank you. Thank you . . . all of you. You have made me feel so supported, so . . . loved. So filled with joy. I feel like I have been reawakened."

The group all rose to their feet. They extinguished the fire and packed up the blankets. Bill carried Annie to Nina's car. Gayle hugged Falcon and whispered, "You believed in me. And now I'm going to honor your confidence in me and spread the message." Falcon hugged her back and wiped a stray tear himself.

Gayle walked to her car. Bill came over to say good-bye.

"What can I say?" she asked. "What you've given me is . . . it defies words."

Bill put up his hand, as if to stop what she was saying. "What I gave you was what Falcon gave me. He says it's in all of us, we've simply misplaced it. All I did was help you find it. And now if you share it, you'll return to the world some of the energy that's been lost in the business climate of today."

"A little Sandbox karma," she laughed.

"Yeah. I guess you could call it that," he joked back.

"Thanks, Bill," Gayle hugged him again.

As she drove home, the scent of the fire, salt air and sea remained in her hair. It lingered and clung to her. She knew Sandbox Wisdom was clinging to her as well, now part of her. And as situations arose, they would be evocative of the past few weeks. Like the fire, the message had energy and power. Like the salt air, the message permeates and provides calmness. And like the sea, the message had a beauty all its own.

Gayle's Journal

* What can I say? We summarized the past few weeks, but what really made it all alive for me was the gathering. When we were all together around the fire, we shared a single language. The wisdom of the Sandbox. If I can spread the word in my department, we can work as a seamless whole, as an inspired crew like Ted's. We could do anything.

* Marshmallows . . . now I'll think of Falcon every time. You know, I had them for DINNER. And that was very child-like. Kids would love a marshmallow dinner. And you know what, life's short. Eat 'em for dinner if you want. ;-)

Chapter Ten

Kindness in words creates confidence. Kindness in thinking creates profoundness. Kindness in giving creates love.

- Lao Tzu

✳

A few months had passed since the beach party for Gayle, when Bill heard from Nina.

"Dad is hoping you can head over to his garage on Friday night."

"Why? What's up?"

A smile crept into Nina's voice, "Oh . . . you know the Falcon."

So it was that Bill was pulling up to Falcon's pristine garage. Quite a few cars were in the front. Usually in the evening, it was just Falcon, alone, working and tinkering. *He's up to something*, Bill mused with a sense of humor. Getting out of his car, he spotted Gayle also getting out of her car a couple of spots down.

"Hey there!" Bill walked toward her and gave her a big, warm hug. They had spoken on the phone several times, but hadn't seen each other since their ocean bonfire.

"Bill," Gayle smiled. "Let me tell you, Falcon is up to something."

"Agreed. How have you been? How are things at work?"

"Excellent! We're setting records for customer service. Records! But it's more than that . . . we get letters. In this day and age, we get hand-signed letters from people telling us what this employee or that employee did to make a difference. Our corporate e-mail is no longer flooded with complaints. Sure, we're still dealing with a lot of the same issues, but Sandbox Wisdom is becoming part of our culture and people are seeing a real difference. They're writing us and saying they didn't think there were companies like us anymore."

"All right!"

"And that's all good stuff, Bill, but get this . . . our people actually _look forward_ to coming to work on Monday. They're eager to share what they did over the weekend with their colleagues, their friends. It's becoming a place where every-one _wants_ to be."

"I know what you mean. I find that many of my people will come in on their day off, just to check out what's going on. To shoot the breeze with friends. We've become an extended family. And since our mobile society places us further from our families of origin . . . and most of us don't live in our hometowns anymore . . . this is a great thing. To have a village to call your own."

Bill and Gayle walked together into Falcon's garage office. Nina was seated in a chair. In front of her were several chairs in a semicircle. Eight to be exact. Six other people were seated and Nina welcomed Bill and Gayle with a smile and a wave. "Those last two chairs are for you, friends."

Nina smiled at the group, "Falcon, my Dad, wanted to gather you eight to share something. He is in the garage with Annie getting it ready. You all know that my Dad saw something special in everyone he's ever met. But there have been a few who, according to him, just seemed to 'get it.' The 'IT' isn't easy to define, but to him, it _is_ easy to see. He says that you can see it in the bright, smiling eyes of a child, and in the playful intelligence of a dolphin. You are those few. Now some of you know each other, and some of you don't. Why don't you all take a minute to introduce yourselves?"

Bill and Gayle introduced themselves, followed by Mr. Garcia, the ice cream parlor owner Bill had met almost two years earlier. Bill winked at him as Mr. Garcia introduced himself.

The next man wore a suit and a smile. Gayle leaned over to Bill and whispered, "Hey! Isn't that . . . "

Bill interrupted, "Sure is! Falcon is a friend and mentor to many prominent people." The man was a high-ranking government official, and Gayle marveled at how the span of Falcon's influence reached to all corners.

There were men and women from all walks of life. A schoolteacher. A firefighter. The man sitting to Bill's left looked familiar to him. Bill leaned over, smiled and shook his hand. "Don't I know you?"

The man replied with a firm handshake and a big, genuine smile, "Mr. West! How are you? You've been a guest at my hotel."

"Gary, right? I thought I recognized you. I haven't seen you out of uniform before. How the heck are you?" Gary was the doorman at one of Bill's favorite hotels. In fact, to Bill, Gary's friendliness and caring attitude embodied the hotel. He WAS the hotel.

After the introductions were made, Nina continued, "I promised my Dad that I wouldn't tell you what I'm about to tell you until he was ready. Well, he feels the time is right." Nina paused to take a breath. "Dad has been living with cancer for the past two years. He refuses to think of it as 'dying.' He says that we're all dying from the day we are born. It's how we live while we're here that counts! Well, the disease has progressed to the point where he must undergo some very aggressive treatment. This may sap a lot of his energy, but not his spirit. You all know him well enough to know that."

Bill and Gayle reeled from the information. Bill guessed that for everyone, Falcon embodied a man who had it all. The material things most of us covet, as well as the non-worldly spirit few of us attain. He was a man filled with faith and inner joy.

"Dad has lived a long, full life. He is really okay with this part of his journey. I don't think any of you would guess that he recently celebrated his eightieth birthday."

"Impossible," Gayle smiled. "That man?"

Nina nodded, "That man. He has been defying people's expectations for him for as long as I can remember."

"With dignity," Mr. Garcia added.

"And a wonderful sense of humor," the man in the suit added.

Nina looked at each of them in turn. "I know this is hard. I've just told you a beloved man is suffering. And Dad does get down from time to time, just like everyone else. But he considers it just part of the drama. He says that the key is to catch yourself, while it's happening, and 'spin' a different story in your mind. Remember, it's your mind, your thoughts, your drama. Make the most of it. You deserve it, and so do all of the people whom you touch during your lifetime. That's his wish for each of you."

A woman who had introduced herself earlier spoke up. "I'm so sorry, Nina. Your father is such a special person." She glanced at the group and continued, "When I first met Falcon, I was a trained engineer resisting a move into sales. I saw it as manipulative, trying to convince people to purchase *my* products. I also experienced a lot of fear . . . of failure, of embarrassment. The very idea of a cold call put me in a cold sweat."

The group chuckled.

The woman looked at Nina and smiled. "Then I met your Dad during one of my first sales calls, and he changed my life. He taught me the vital importance of sales, and he taught me to eliminate my fears, by focusing on the other person's feelings; their expectation and concerns. He helped me to see outside the box and to realize that sales can be a very creative and helpful profession, if I truly work to understand everyone's feelings about the future, and how I can help improve it for them. At first I thought his advice was a little touchy-feely, but after discovering that Falcon was a trained engineer like myself, and after practicing his philosophy in the 'real world', I was convinced. Keeping others feelings in the forefront of your mind isn't simply sentimentalism. It's a very pragmatic approach to business, albeit a difficult one to master. Falcon has been my friend and teacher ever since that first 'sales' meeting. I couldn't admire anyone more."

"I know you all love him," Nina smiled. "And now . . . he's waiting for us."

Bill spotted Annie first. She was in the garage, blowing bubbles, and helping Grandpa. Party streamers hung from the ceiling. Oldies music boomed from a vintage jukebox. Gayle smiled. The bubbles were gently floating down, bouncing off

off the glistening, candy-colored cars. Feeling a heaviness tug at her heart, she realized that children learn that bubbles are to be enjoyed, that you can't grasp them. *Life is the same way,* Gayle thought. *I need to live life that way, like Falcon has.*

Falcon emerged from, where else, under the hood of a car. A beautiful, baby blue, 1955 Chrysler New Yorker convertible. He went over to his eight friends and embraced each one. A couple of tears were shed, but the hugs and handshakes were warm and full of genuine respect and compassion.

"OK, now . . . no sadness. Just life. Embrace it! I want to honor each of you, my treasured friends, by giving you one of my restored, classic cars." Annie handed out the keys, along with drawings she made for everyone.

"You may use Annie's beautiful drawings of your car to locate it and . . . climb in!"

Bill and Gayle looked at their keys and drawings. They were both stunned. The entire group was. Yet Falcon was almost ecstatic with the idea of giving each of them one of his treasures. His enthusiasm was infectious. The group was soon whooping and hollering, and laughing and dancing. Bill's car was the white Corvette whose hubcap his people had found nearly two years ago. Bill mused that this was coming full circle in a way. Climbing behind the wheel, he noticed a note on the seat next to him. *Please take care of it for me. Embrace it, add to it, share it. It's in the glove compartment.* He opened the glove box to find Falcon's quote book. He was stunned and honored.

Annie came over to the car and climbed in the front seat.

"Hi, Annie."

"Hi, Mr. West."

"I like your picture."

"Thank you. I do too," she grinned.

"Pretty amazing of your Grandpa to do this. Give away his cars."

"They're just things he loves for people he loves. You know, Mr. West, when you die, your spirit goes into all the people whose lives you've touched. That way you live with them always."

"I know that now, Annie. And you're pretty amazing to know that already." Bill lovingly rubbed her hair.

Annie smiled and absorbed his compliment.

Bill heard Falcon reassembling everyone.

"I trust you're all happy with your cars."

Gary laughed. "Mr. Falcon, this is a day for the history books!"

"Well, my friends, you deserve all of this and more. You are all true leaders. You have taken the risk of opening yourselves to others. You've brought a shared sense of spirit, passion and fun to your communities and organizations. You've learned how to bring together the contribution of others, while bringing out the best of everyone. It's this way of being that sets you eight apart."

He walked around the circle looking at each of them. "Leaders stimulate the shared values of Sandbox Wisdom from person to person. They teach a way of thinking, which is one of the most difficult things a leader must do. Why? Because there are no recipes. It's your personal style, along with your desire to learn and change and make a difference."

Coming to Bill, he smiled. He poked Bill gently in the chest with his finger and said, "Always listen to your heart, Bill. It's what's in *here* that counts."

Bill smiled. "You got it, Falcon."

They all listened attentively. They were trying to absorb his message, as if they had a mission. They *did* have a mission.

"True leaders never try to acquire success and fame at the expense of others. They're other focused and lead through influence. And they don't choose their destiny. Their destiny chooses them. You are a group of people living together at this unique time. How you communicate this wisdom, and care for each other, means everything."

The eight of them looked around at each other, saying with their eyes, *Of course, we'll be there for each other.*

"Because of the frantic pace today, most people have lost their sense of helping others, of making a contribution. You are all a gift to others. And when things get hard, as they inevitably will, accept the fact that you may not know why. Listen to others opinions, thank them and smile. Then continue to do YOUR work."

Falcon clasped Gary's hand to the man next to him.

"Find yourself a buddy. And when you find yourself sliding back, call this Sandbox buddy."

Bill instinctively reached for Gayle's hand.

"No matter what happens," Falcon smiled, "we'll always be friends. Now take your beautiful cars, and go out there and make a difference in the world. Then I will know I have really succeeded. As Emerson wrote, 'To know one life has breathed easier because you have lived . . . this is to have succeeded.'"

Bill hugged Falcon good-bye. "I want to thank you for giving me the best thing in my life. You've changed me forever. You've done that."

Falcon just hugged his friend. "You did that, Bill."

"But I couldn't have without you."

Bill hugged Nina and Annie good-bye and stepped towards his Corvette to wait for Gayle as she said her private good-byes and thank you's, as well.

With tears in her eyes, Nina walked over to where Bill stood and whispered. "Take a look around at all of his stuff. From his cars to his magic to philosophy, my Dad is the consummate Jack-of-all-Trades. But you know, Bill, he always wanted to master something. To be the *best* at something."

Bill looked her in the eyes. "Nina, he *is* the best. Emerson also wrote that 'God evidently does not intend us all to be rich, or powerful, or great, but He does intend us all to be friends.' Your Dad is the *best* friend anyone could ever hope for."

Gayle joined them. "I can't believe the roller coaster of emotions I am experiencing right now. He's such a wonderful person. He's helped so many people with his wisdom. Exponentially, that number must be huge."

"You know," said Bill, "I heard a saying once, that when an old man dies an entire library burns to the ground. We have to make sure to take that strand of Falcon that is weaved throughout the fabric of our lives and weave it into others."

"We have our work cut out for us," Gayle said.

Bill climbed into his mint condition, classic Corvette. "We do. But we had the best teacher of them all." He slowly pulled out of the garage and Gayle laughed as he drove away. There on his license plate . . . SANDBOX.

GAYLE'S JOURNAL

* Life is to be enjoyed . . . Dance!!!

CLOSING THOUGHTS

Vision doesn't mean dreams and ideals for the future.
It means understand life as it is, of what we are,
of what we are doing.

- Alan Watts

✳

*W*atts also wrote that without this understanding, "it is simply ridiculous to talk of being practical and getting results." My mission is to help you *get* those results by engaging you in transformational lectures, workshops and seminars; by exposing you to new ideas, new solutions, and new inspiration.

So, if you are an organizational leader, cultural creative or change agent and you're ready to move beyond limiting beliefs, ready to open yourself to the possibility of radically improving your relationships with others and achieving outstanding business effectiveness, I would love the opportunity to help.

I'd also love to hear your thoughts regarding the ideas put forth in this book. It is through open and honest debate that we find our own meaning and form insights which will improve our personal lives, organizations, families, and communities. Please contact me directly by sending an email to **tom@sandboxwisdom.com**.

Good luck during your personal journey. Let this Hindustani proverb be your guiding light: "The adult looks to deed, the child to love."